A BIBLIOGRAPHY of COMPUTER MUSIC

A BIBLIOGRAPHY of COMPUTER MUSIC
A Reference for Composers
SANDRA L. TJEPKEMA

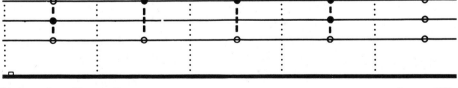

University of Iowa Press

Iowa City

Tjepkema, Sandra L., 1953-
   A bibliography of computer music.

   Includes index.
   1. Computer Music — Bibliography.   I.   Title.
ML128.E4T55   016.789'7   81-2967
ISBN 0-87745-110-9   AACR2

University of Iowa Press, Iowa City
© 1981 by The University of Iowa. All rights reserved
Printed in the United States of America

This book is dedicated especially to those musicians who grew up cherishing certain favorite phonograph records, those records being an earlier meeting of music and modern technology that has made all the difference.

Contents

Preface

The increasing presence of computers of every size
is well known. Less well perceived in many quarters is
the spread of this technology into the music world in
both commercial and experimental applications. Microprocessors (i.e. small computers whose central processing unit is contained in one integrated circuit "chip")
are now being used in many common appliances, office
equipment, and, closer to our concerns here, in professional audio equipment, new electronic instruments being
marketed commercially, and even in musical toys designed
for children. Historical eras can be defined by basic
changes in the tools in use, that is the technology
developed and brought into widespread use by people in
a particular time. The computer, however employed, is
undoubtedly such an era-defining tool.

It may be instructive then to look to the past for
comparisons in the relation of a society's tools in a
given period to its culture and arts. In general, it can
be seen that when a new technology has been applied to
the means of distribution of art, music, and literature,
an enormous change has occurred in the general availa-
bility of artistic products, resulting in a change in
the very role of the arts in that society. This has also
affected the approach that artists might take, given the
new potential audience and the characteristics of the new
medium in which the work will be made and/or received.

For instance, the effect of the printing press
on literature (and music) is undisputed. As a result,

literature, formerly a rare pleasure for the few, became more widely available and assumed many new forms, among them the popular novel and the newspaper. Literature then had potentially a larger audience, and at the same time, many more small specialized ones, rather than the small and quite homogeneous one as before. The Xerox machine has most certainly accelerated this effect. Where before, everyone could be a reader, now everyone can be his own publisher. Likewise, music can be hand copied, printed, or xeroxed, and distributed to popular or specialized audiences.

Beyond this, sound recordings made it possible to preserve and/or publish musical performances themselves. The parallel development can be seen in the boom in popular music and the development of separate labels for recordings of interest to much smaller audiences. Folk music, jazz, classical music, and contemporary music in the classical vein are in this second category. This state of affairs could be seen as the natural outcome of the advent of sound recording and its expansion as a low-cost commodity available to nearly everyone.

The distribution of music may be further affected by the application of digital techniques to the printing and recording of music. There are several programs under development or in use at present for extremely efficient printing of music. Digital techniques have been employed by Stockham and others in sound recording, with spectacular results. An upheaval in the recording industry may be in the making. Furthermore, there are now on the market several computer programs for music instruction, recorded on cassettes for use with home computer systems. It remains to be seen if more sophisticated music programs (or perhaps musical game programs) are seen to offer commercial gain and so become widespread. The desk-top size computer may well become a popular adjunct to the hi-fi set-up and the television for home entertainment, as commonplace as the piano in homes of the last century. New and stimulating material of an aural sort may be in demand for such systems, as once easy sonatas were for amateur pianists. Amateur musical composition activity and private exchange of the resulting creations may well be enhanced by such a development. The diversity of modern music (much discussed as it is) may be augmented, but this is not necessarily cause for lament.

In all these cases, it might be expected that artists would want to take into their own hands the means of propagating their work and use the unique properties of the medium to produce a separate kind of experience. This is directly analogous to the development of film, which at first merely recorded events as they usually occurred on the stage and later began to assume a character of its own. Similarly, recorded music is a different experience from the concert hall performance, and carries with it, potentially, a different artistic meaning.

The use of computers for generation of sound to be stored and reproduced on magnetic tape is very much an extension of electronic music on tape, and thus of recorded music in general, and therefore takes on some of its characteristics. In one extrapolation of this comparison, one might conclude that the means of presenting the finished work should be reconsidered. If recorded music is to be presented in public rather than simply sold as reproduced objects or perhaps even limited edition serials, the setting should be other than the conventional concert hall, a corollary to the cinema or TV room (if in fact the music isn't already accompanying one of these forms or being used as part of a theatrical production).

Also, the fact remains that the standard orchestral instruments are essentially the same as those used in the nineteenth century, and are perhaps best suited to music which accepts their built-in predispositions. In recognizing this, composers might collaborate more happily with instrumentalists, who are, of course, devoted to their instruments and the existing body of musical literature written for them. On the other hand, composers whose approaches include quarter-tones and other tunings, very exacting rhythmic structures or timbral transformations, or extremes of dynamic or pitch range (unknown to that age of moderation that

produced the modern flute, clarinet, piano, etc.) might
find that a programmable sound synthesis system is
better suited to their intentions than any orchestral
instrument.

In addition to these specific aims, the electronic
mediums, i.e. tape or discs as storage mechanisms for
compositions, have expressive qualities in common
peculiar to themselves which a composer might find
attractive. One of these is a feeling of intimacy with
the audience that is unprecedented. The composer can
literally whisper into the listener's ear, especially
if the listener is wearing headphones. This quality
has been recognized before in television and in radio,
of course. This effect contrasts greatly, however, with
that of public statement or even heroics that one asso-
ciates with orchestra performances.

Aside from these considerations, both traditional
sound producing phenomena and all sound producing
technology ought to be the proper domain of musicians.
Tape recorders, radios, telephones, analog and digital
oscillators, and digital sound synthesis are all legit-
imate areas for musical investigation, for in all of
these we may have tools for music making. In the small
computer particularly, we have a versatile tool which
is rapidly becoming more available, inexpensive, and
portable. It might be well to remember that the word
"instrument" as used outside of music conveys the sense
of "tool." The mystique of violins that we have
cultivated makes us forget this. In carrying out some
musical ideas, an electronic tool may better serve.

        *   *   *   *   *

In the early days of photography, the conventional
argument against its claims to art had to do with the
idea that the device did too much for the practitioner,
that the skill in pointing a camera and pressing a
button was not great. Electronic music has often been
subject to the same abusive argument. One cannot exactly

claim that it takes no skill to program a small computer
to do any sort of task, but the notion that the computer
is doing most of the composer's aesthetic work seems
firmly rooted. It is not commonly recognized, in other
situations as well, that the use of computers does not
necessarily imply total automation. Generally, in casual
discussions of music it is exceedingly easy to trivial-
ize any means of music-making: toot a horn, beat a drum,
fiddle around, plunk out a tune, twist a knob, etc.
However, in spite of all that has been said about button
pushing, we have found that photographs can indeed
communicate something aesthetically siginificant to us,
and that the determining factor in their effectiveness
is not the camera itself, but the photographer's choice
of subject, point of view, and technical expertise.
Furthermore, photographs, with their seeming mirror-like
image of the world, play upon us in a most intriguing
and evocative way. This image, in fact, is subject to
considerable manipulation, depending on the photographer's intent. Sound recordings act upon us in a similar
way. The computer already figures in the present battery
of professional audio equipment for manipulating sonic
images taken from actual performances. Instances of this
may be found in the automated mixdown of elaborately
produced pop tunes in commercial recording studios, as
well as in various types of experimental musical efforts,
and in the programmed reconstruction of musical sounds
for study purposes. The degree of manipulation or distortion of recorded material is merely a matter of choice--
it is in the very nature of recording (or, in a broader
context, information science). For this reason, I would
think that any composer, and in fact any musician, would
want to explore this area to some extent. Sound generation and sound manipulation (or sound processing) are
his business.

Finally, it seems universally agreed that artists
do well to make art of the materials at hand. At this
point, IC's (integrated circuits) would almost seem to
be a basic material in our culture, at least in the
United States. Perhaps electronic instruments, including
the computer, may prove to be the basis for a unique

music of unmistakably American character, as typical in its way as is aircraft design, fifties-style automobiles, and such examples of American industrial design as CocaCola bottles. These visual examples are evidence of a sensibility that does not have much to do with nineteenth century Europe, and this music, in building on that sensibility, could perhaps achieve a similar kind of classicism on its own terms.

*   *   *   *   *

This bibliography is intended to be a comprehensive listing of books, articles, dissertations, and papers relating to the use of computers by composers of music. Also included are a number of published and unpublished users' manuals for sound synthesis programs at various installations and for systems which make use of programmed controls with analog or digital sound generating devices. The material was chosen from the point of view of a composer interested in these developments. It was therefore restricted to creative applications relating to (1) generation of musical structures which are to be transcribed into common musical notation; (2) performance of lower level compositional tasks as an aid to the composer; (3) investigations of the creative process in music which involve the use of computer programming; (4) digital sound synthesis as an end unto itself and as a means of realizing musical ideas; (5) the use of programmed controls for some compositional end. This compilation excludes the synthesis of prototypes of folk tunes, hymns, and the like, and the synthesis of speech unless used for some musical purpose. Although such activities are of interest to the composer who would make use of digital technology, they are somewhat tangential to the musical/creative objectives of the work which is documented here.

For the purposes of this bibliography, "computer" will be defined as a device which is programmable and which gives output in binary code. In recent years, a number of devices have been designed which make use of digital technology, i.e. "intelligent" terminals,

programmable calculators, and digital oscillators;
hence there is now only a fine line between what might
be called a computer and what is not. The ambiguity
may be further appreciated by realizing that in varying
degrees instructions in a computer program may be
replaced by specifically designed processors. There
are tradeoffs then between the complexity of the program
(i.e. software) and the amount of electronic circuitry
(i.e. hardware). Among the products of the computer
industry there are now a great number of different
combinations of hardware and software, weighted one
way or the other. Along with hybrid systems of analog
and digital control devices, mixed digital systems have
been built which make use of a computer controlling a
digital oscillator. The emphasis in such systems is on
more programming and less hardware.

The category of devices as defined above then
excludes such instruments as the RCA synthesizer and
the Siemens synthesizer, both of which are programmable
by means of punched paper tape but give analog output.
These instruments are important historically, and the
many discussions of the RCA synthesizer in particular
have been listed in bibliographies of electronic music.
Also excluded are microprocessors in which logic has
been pre-set by the manufacturer. These are not programmable but dedicated to a specific use, such as the control
mechanism in microwave ovens and some new models of
electronic organs. Product reviews and technical writings
on the design of computer-related equipment are also
excluded, along with the topics of printing of musical
scores by computer and the burgeoning field of digital
recording. The computer models under discussion here
include large, high-speed installations such as the
IBM 7090, IBM 360, CDC 6600, PDP 10, and the Sigma 7;
smaller computers such as the PDP 11, PDP 15, and the
GE 635; and, more recently, microprocessors such as
the Intel 8080 series, MOS Technology 6502, and the
Motorola 6800. (See list of manufaturers [p. 246] for
further information on the computer types to which
reference is made in this bibliography.)

The works listed, which include materials dated

from 1956 through January 1979, range widely in nature
from general introductions to "computer music" (intended
for musicians, engineers, programmers, or computer
hobbyists) to very technical reports on research in
progress. Also, since many articles deal with several
aspects of the subject, it was not deemed useful to
divide the listings into separate classifications. An
index has been provided for easy reference by the reader
to specific topics. A short list of commonly used
acronyms has been included for those not familiar with
the conventions of computer science literature.

Every effort has been made to inspect each item
listed and provide annotations. Where this has been
impossible, only the item has been listed. Since many
papers containing significant information in this field
are unpublished manuscripts, as many of these as possible
have been cited, along with the printed abstracts that
appear in professional journals. Dissertations have
been provided with University Microfilm numbers wherever
possible, as well as citations of the abstract published
in *Dissertation Abstracts.*

Other bibliographies consulted in compiling the
present one include Lowell Cross's *Bibliography of
Electronic Music,* Hugh Davies's *Répertoire International
des Musiques Electroacoustiques/ International Electronic Music Catalogue,* annual bibliographies published in
the periodical *Computers and the Humanities,* the bibliographies of Peter Bahler, Gary Berlind, Stefan Kostka,
and Marc Battier, the *Répertoire International des
Musiques Éxperimentales,* as well as the *Music Index,*
*Abstracts of Music Literature: Répertoire International
de la Littérature Musicale* (RILM), *Reader's Guide to
Periodical Literature,* and the indexes to the *Journal
of the Audio Engineering Society, Journal of the Acoustical Society of America,* and the *Journal of the Institute of Electronic and Electrical Engineering.*

I am grateful to Lowell Cross for his careful
reading of the manuscript, suggestions on matters of
style and documentation, and the loan of materials from
his personal library. I also wish to thank Peter Lewis
for acquainting me with the computer music activities

of Leo Kupper and others in France, and for the loan of various documents. I owe a debt of gratitude to Cleve Scott, on whose suggestion this project was begun in 1974, and who helped me to obtain copies of conference proceedings that I had missed.

Thanks also to the personnel of the libraries at the University of Iowa, Yale University, the IBM Corporation Research Center at Yorktown, New York, and the University of Illinois, Indiana University, the Magnavox Corporation, and Ball State University.

More than thanks are due to my husband Thomas Mintner, who served as my sounding board, whose professional expertise I called upon with my questions on professional audio and other matters, and whose constant encouragement saw me through to the end of this project.

S. T.
Danbury, Conn.
February 1981

A Bibliography of Computer Music

1. Abbott, Alain. "Approche de composition d'une œuvre électroacoustique." *Conférence des Journées d'Etudes Festival International du Son.* Paris: Editions Radio, 1973.

   General remarks concerning compositional uses of technology. Illustrations included.

2. Abbott, Curtis. "Magazine review." *Computer Music Journal* 2, 2 (Sept. 1978), 7-8.

   Review of two publications which are devoted to the subject of scales and intonations other than the twelve-tone equal-tempered one and which contain theoretical information that may be used in computer programs for music. The publications are *Xenharmonikon* and *Interval: A Microtonal Newsletter.*

3. _____. "Machine Tongues I." *Computer Music Journal* 2, 1 (July 1978), 4-5.

   Explanation of a programming language called C for use with a PDP-11 operating system, for the benefit of 'computer musicians' (expected to be novices at programming).

4. _____. "Machine Tongues II." *Computer Music Journal* 2, 2 (Sept. 1978), 4-6.

Discussion of the idea of formal procedure and current practice for specifying program code. References are listed.

5. _____. "Machine Tongues III." *Computer Music Journal* 2, 3 (Dec. 1978), 7-9.

Discussion of data and data structures for the uninitiated. Terms are defined and characteristic programming techniques are explained. A simple example of an application of these ideas to programmed music-making is offered.

6. _____. "A software approach to interactive processing of musical sound." *Computer Music Journal* 2, 1 (July 1978), 19-23.

Description of a program called INV, intended to perform mixing and editing operations digitally, and also various test routines. The author presents the program as a lesson in approaching software problems of this type.

7. Ahl, David H. "Software technology music system." *Creative Computing* 3, 5 (Sept.-Oct. 1977), 96-100.

A simple kit for the computer hobbyist is described. The kit includes a small printed circuit board and cassette tape; the assembled kit may be plugged into a hi-fi system. Tunes may be transcribed and programmed.

8. Alles, H.G. "A modular approach to building large digital synthesis systems." *Computer Music Journal* 1, 4 (Nov. 1977), 10-13.

   Also, presented at the 1977 International Computer Music Conference, held at the Center for Music Experiment and Related Research, University of California, San Diego, Cal.

   A series of four one-card special purpose processors to be combined arbitrarily is described here. These four modules are the oscillator module (described in detail by the author and P. diGiugno elsewhere), filter module, reverberation module, and switch module. The resulting large system may be controlled by a multiple LSI-11 computing system or the larger PDP-11 (both made by D.E.C.).

9. _____. "A portable digital sound synthesis system." *Computer Music Journal* 1, 4 (Nov. 1977), 5-6.

   Also, presented at the 1977 International Computer Music Conference, held at the Center for Music Experiment and Related Research, University of California, San Diego.

   A system under development at Bell Laboratories and at IRCAM (Institut de Recherche et Coordination Acoustique/Musique) is described. An LSI-11 computing system is interfaced for data input from two touch-sensitive organ-type manuals, four 'joysticks,' and 72 levers. The microprocessor is the main control-device with the digital synthesizer (a multiplexed oscillator bank designed by diGiugno and Alles) as the sound source. Storage is available on floppy disks.

10. _____. A real-time all-digital music synthesis system. Paper presented at the
58th convention of the Audio Engineering
Society, New York, Nov. 4-7, 1977.

A real-time digital synthesis system small
enough to be portable is described. It includes a floppy disc-based computing system,
64 oscillators, 32 filters, 256 envelope-
generators, a programmable digital delay,
and a switch matrix. Performer interface
provides touch-sensitive keys, slide-levers,
and a joystick.

11. _____. "A 256-channel performer input device."
Computer Music Journal 1, 4 (Nov. 1977),
14-15.

The performer interface, intended to be
used with a digital synthesizer (see above
article) and LSI-11 computing system, is
described here. Technical description of
position-sensitive keys on the keyboard,
as well as the means by which data is
encoded from the keyboard, is offered.

12. _____. See DiGiugno and Alles.

13. Allouis, Jean-François. "Syter." *Cahiers recherche/
musique* [Paris: Institut National de
l'Audio-visuel and Groupe de Recherches
Musicales] 1, 3 (1976), 62-91.

A multiprocessor system called SYTER
(synthèse digitale temps réel) is described.
The system allows natural sounds to be
converted to digital signals, manipulated
and transformed, then re-converted to
audio signals.

14. Alonso, Sidney; Jon Appleton; and Cameron Jones. "A computer music system for every university: the Dartmouth College example." *Creative Computing* 3, 2 (1977), 57-59.

The use of a digital synthesizer in a college environment for composing, aural skills training, and performance of composition exercises is described.

15. _____. "Description d'un système digital specifique pour l'enseignement, la composition et l'execution de musique." *Faire* [Bourges: Editions GMEB] 2-3 (1975), 60-67.

Also, appears as "A special purpose digital system for musical instruction, composition, and performance." *Computers and the Humanities* 10, 4 (July-Aug. 1976), 209-215.

Also, as "A special purpose digital system for the instruction, composition, and performance of music." In *Proceedings of the 1975 Conference on Computers in the Undergraduate Curricula*. Fort Worth, Texas: Texas Christian University, Department of Computer Science, 1975. 17-22.

A digital synthesizer developed at Dartmouth College which employs a minicomputer linked with the large Dartmouth timesharing system DTSS, is described here. The sound source is provided by digital oscillators, forming an eight-channel system. The synthesizer is used for composing, aural skills training, and for performance of composition exercises written by students at Dartmouth College.

16. Amuedo, John W. Spiral: a signal processing
    research language. Paper presented at
    the First International Conference on
    Computer Music, Massachussetts Institute
    of Technology, Oct. 28-31, 1976.

    Description of a language for interactive
    real-time sound generation with a system
    that uses the Floating Point Systems
    AP-120B Array Processor. Sound signals are
    uniquely defined and associated with a
    repertoire of signal transformations.

17. Andersen, Kurt H. "A digital sound generation unit."
    *Electronic Music and Musical Acoustics:
    Annual Report* [Aarhus: University of Aarhus
    Institute of Musicology] 2 (1976), 25.

    Detailed hardware description of the digital
    sound generator of the EGG synthesizer,
    which is built up from multiple 'voices,'
    each of which generates a tone from its
    own waveform buffer through a D/A converter
    and filter. The device has been in practical
    use, but still has some problems.

18. _____. "A digital sound synthesizer keyboard."
    *Electronic Music and Musical Acoustics:
    Annual Report* [Aarhus: University of Aarhus
    Institute of Musicology] 2 (1976), 5.

    Updated and revised version appears as
    "A digital sound synthesizer keyboard."
    Computer Music Journal 2, 3 (Dec. 1978),
    16-23.

Information on the hardware construction
and operation of a touch-sensitive keyboard
as an input device for the EGG synthesizer,
under development at the University of Aarhus,
Denmark. The motion of each key is tracked
by means of a coded film-strip and photo-cells
with a digital electronic scanning system.
Diagrams and photographs are included, plus
a list of articles published on this synthesizer's various features.

19. Andriessen, Louis; Leo Geurts; and Lambert Meertens.
"Componist en computer." *De Gids* 132 (1969),
304–311.

Introductory articles on the use of computers
by composers.

20. "Annual bibliography for 1973 and supplement to
preeceeding years: music." *Computers and the
Humanities* 8, 2 (1974), 108–110.

21. "Annual bibliography for 1974 and supplement to
preeceeding years: music." *Computers and the
Humanities* 9, 3 (1975), 141–142.

22. "Annual bibliography for 1975 and supplement to
preeceeding years: music." *Computers and the
Humanities* 10, 2 (1976), 120–121.

23. "Annual bibliography for 1976 and supplement to
preeceeding years: music." *Computers and the
Humanities* 11, 2 (1977), 117–118.

24. "Annual bibliography for 1977 and supplement to
preeceeding years: music." *Computers and the
Humanities* 13, 2 (1979), 181–182.

25. This item deleted.

26. Appleton, Jon. "Aesthetic direction in electronic music." *Western Humanities Review* 18 (1964), 345-350.

27. _____. "New role for the composer." *Music Journal* 27, 3 (March 1969), 28, 59-61.

    Swedish translation appears in *Nutida Musik* 13, 4 (1969-70), 38-41.

    Also, appears in Eng., Fr., and Ger. in *World of Music* 13, 1 (1971), 29-40.

    An overall look is taken at the impact of new technology, including computers, on the philosophical orientation of the composer.

28. _____. Problems of designing a composer's language for digital synthesis. Paper presented at the 57th convention of the Audio Engineering Society, Los Angeles, May 10-13, 1977. Preprint No. 1230.

    The Dartmouth digital synthesizer is discussed, and the point is made that more composers may use such devices provided that the programming language is accessible to those who have never studied acoustics or programming.

29. _____; and Ronald Perera, eds. *The Development and Practice of Electronic Music.* Englewood Cliffs, N.J.: Prentice-Hall, 1975.

    Textbook of electronic music, including an essay by John Rogers, "The uses of digital computers in electronic music." See Rogers.

30. "À propos de l'ordinateur dans la musique."
    Le Monde de la Musique 9, 3 (1967), 10.

31. "À propos des mécanismes de création esthétique."
    Extrait de Cybernética no. 2. Namur: Assoc-
    iation Internationale de Cybernétique, 1967.

32. Arfib, Daniel. Digital synthesis of complex
    spectra by means of multiplication of
    non-linear distorted sine waves. Paper
    presented to the 59th convention of the
    Audio Engineering Society, Hamburg, Feb. 28-
    March 3, 1978. Preprint No. 1319.

    The simulation by computer of a saturated
    amplifier (in order to produce extra har-
    monics) has already been used by J.-C. Risset
    to produce clarinet-like sounds. The author
    has elaborated upon this model, adding
    amplitude modulation to produce a variety
    of spectra.

33. Armbruster, Greg. *"Ripples."* *Computer Music
    Journal* 1, 3 (June 1977), 40-47.

    Description of the author's work for
    computer-controlled synthesizer, *Ripples.*
    Complete score is included.

34. Ashford, T.H. See Kobrin and Ashford.

35. Ashton, Alan C. "A computer stores, composes,
    and plays music." *Computers and Automation*
    20, 12 (Dec. 1971), 43.

    An electronic player-organ, driven by a
    small computer, has been designed at the
    University of Utah. The computer accepts
    input from the organ keyboard or in code.
    It has been used by students for playback-
    performance of orchestra scores.

36. _____. Electronics, music, and computers.
Diss., University of Utah, 1970. 183 pp.
*UM*71-3987. *Dissertation Abstracts* 31
(1970), 4627B.

Survey of electronic music and the use of
computers in the electronic music studio.

37. Asuar, José Vicente. "Musica con computadores:
come hacerlo . . . ?" *Revista Musical
Chilena* 26, 118 (1972), 33-66.

Discussion of the use of the computer in
musical composition and its justification.
A description and analysis of the first
computer music in Chile, *FORMAS I*, is
given.

38. _____. Programmed control of analog sound
generators. National Science Foundation
Project No. GK-14191 Technical Report No.
5, Buffalo, N.Y., Jan. 1973. 46 pp. Mimeo.

39. _____. "La segunda generación de música
electrónica." *Revista Musical Chilena*
26, 134 (April-Sept. 1976), 75-110.

40. Attneave, Fred. "Stochastic composition processes."
Journal of Aesthetics and Art Criticism
17 (1959), 503-510.

41. Attree, Richard. "Wee also have sound-houses."
Sound International 1, 3 (July 1978), 61.

Discussion of MUSIC V as implemented at
City University of New York, with modifications by Stanley Haynes there. The program
runs on an ICL 1905E computer currently.
(Title of article taken from Francis Bacon.)

42. Austin, Larry. *"Caritas."* *Source: Music of the Avant-Garde* 8, 4 (1970), 42.

The composer describes his work *Caritas*: sound materials realized with a PDP-10 computer at Stanford University were subjected to modification by a Buchla synthesizer, producing ten channels of sound. Each channel was routed to transducers attached to aluminum sculptures. A recording is included with this issue.

43. _____. Composing hybrid music with an open, interactive system. Paper presented at the First International Conference on Computer Music, Massachussetts Institute of Technology, Oct. 28-31, 1976.

The digital/analog system called SYCOM, at the University of South Florida, is described. The process of exploring new materials within such a system, eventually working them into an idiom of one's own, is described.

44. _____. *"HPSCHD."* *Source: Music of the Avant-Garde* 4, 2 (July 1968), 10-19.

Also, appears in *Nutida Musik* 13, 4 (1969-70), 16-25.

Also, included in National Science Foundation Project No. GK-14191 Technical Report No. 4, Buffalo, N.Y., Aug. 1972. 205-213.

John Cage and Lejaren Hiller are interviewed concerning their composition *HPSCHD*. A part of the flowchart of the program and print-out of several files are included.

45. _____. "SYCOM-- systems complex for the studio
and performing arts." *Numus West* [Mercer
Island, Washington] 1, 5 (1974), 57-59.

Description of new facilities at the
University of South Florida, which include
a PDP 11/10 computer, D/A and A/D converters,
interfaced with various types of analog
equipment (Moog and Buchla synthesizers).
The teaching and research program there
is also described.

46. _____; and Larry Bryant. "A computer-synchron-
ized, multi-track recording system." in
Information Processing Systems, Proceed-
ings of the Second Annual Music Computation
Conference, Nov. 7-9, 1975, part 4. Urbana:
University of Illinois, 1975. 1-12.

Description of a recording system under
development at the University of South
Florida, for the purpose of realizing the
percussion 'layer' of Ives' *Universe
Symphony,* part of the author's continuing
project of completing Ives' work. Austin
also mentions his own *Three Fantasies on
Ives' Universe Symphony.*

47. Bachman, Claus-Henning. "Musik und Computer in den
U.S.A." *Schweizerische Musikzeitung/Revue
Musicale Suisse* 116, 1 (Jan.-Feb. 1976),
30-32.

48. Baecker, Ronald. See Buxton, Reeves, Baecker,
and Mezer.

49. Bahler, Peter B. Electronic and computer music:
an annotated bibliography of writings in
English. Thesis, University of Rochester,
1966. 128 pp.

50. Baker, Robert. MUSICOMP, a music simulator-
    interpreter for compositional procedures
    for the IBM 7090 electronic digital computer.
    University of Illinois Experimental Music
    Studio Technical Report No. 9, Urbana, July
    1963. 44 pp.

    Users' manual for MUSICOMP, a programming
    language developed at the University of
    Illinois for generating compositional
    structures as specified by subroutines.

51. _____. Preparation of musicwriter punched
    paper tapes for use by the Illiac digital
    computer. University of Illinois Experi-
    mental Music Studio Technical Report No. 2,
    Urbana, June 1961. 14 pp.

52. _____. See Hiller and Baker.

53. Bamberger, Jeanne. Capturing intuitive knowledge
    in procedural descriptions. Paper presented
    at the First International Conference on
    Computer Music, Massachussetts Institute of
    Technology, Oct. 28-31, 1976.

    The composer's basic interaction with
    computer music systems in creative pursuits,
    is examined.

54. Barbaud, Pierre. "Ars nova." *Autotisme* 15, 9
    (Sept. 1970), 423-428.

    The author emphasizes aesthetic considerations
    in the use of computers in music-making and
    the need for such music to be conceived
    outside the terms of the nineteenth century.

55. _____. "Avenement de la musique cybernetique."
    Les Lettres Nouvelles 7, 8 (April 22, 1959),
    28. Introductory article.

56. _____. "Composing music and generating sound by computer." *Information Processing '74*, Proceedings of the IFIP Congress, 1974. Amsterdam: North Holland Co., 1974.

Report on digital synthesis to date.

57. _____. "Highlights of some magnificent principles." *Page: Bulletin of the Computer Arts Society* 28 (Jan. 1973), 2.

Mathematical models for composition are described.

58. _____. *Initiation à la composition musicale automatique*. Paris: Dunod, 1966. 106 pp.

Detailed description of an early composition which involved the use of a computer, *Imprévisibles nouveautés*, produced in 1961 by Barbaud and Blanchard at the Centre de Calcul Electronique de la Compaignie des Machines Bull. It utilized the twelve-tone technique: a row was generated at random by the computer and modified according to various combinatorial operations and standard permutations, as specified by the program. The output was then transcribed into common musical notation. Sample programs are included.

59. _____. "Méthodes d'analyse de textes harmoniques." *Informatique Musicale, Journées d'Etudes Oct. 1973. Textes des Conférences*. Paris: C.N.R.S., 1973. 165-176.

The author's theory of composition, which he has used to create programs for music, is discussed, along with the application of probability and group theory in music.

60. _____. "Musique algorithmique." *Esprit* 28,
    280 (Jan. 1960), 92-97.

    Also appears in *Bulletin Technique de la
    Compaignie des Machines Bull* 2 (1961), 22.

    Discussion of the application of mathematics
    to music, and the author's own work.

61. _____. *La Musique, discipline scientifique*.
    Paris: Dunod, 1968. 153 pp.

    The aesthetic and theoretical groundwork is
    laid for the use of information theory and
    group theory in musical composition, and for
    the use of computers as a means for realizing
    such ideas.

62. _____; and R. Blanchard. "Musique algorithm-
    ique." *La Revue Musicale*, special issue,
    June 1960.

    Imprévisibles nouveautés is discussed, and
    a recording of the work is enclosed with the
    issue.

63. Barbour, J. Murray. "Comment on 'Aid to music com-
    position employing a random probability sys-
    tem.'" *Journal of the Acoustical Society
    of America* 34, 1 (1962), 128-129.

    Comment on the work of Olson and Belar and
    their "composing machine." Casual treatment
    of general rhythmic and formal qualities of
    S. Foster's music by the machine, in its
    simulation of Foster-prototypes, are pointed
    out.

64. Barraud, J. "Musique et ordinateurs." *La Revue Musicale* 257 (1963), 9-12.

Examination of popular attitudes toward the computer and toward music vs. the fresh attitudes that Iannis Xenakis brings to both.

65. Batel, Günther. "Über die Komponenten der Musik: Eine statistische Untersuchung in der Musikpsychologie." *R.E.L.O. Revue* 4 (1976), 13-35.

66. Barton, David K. See Hemingway and Barton.

67. Battier, Marc. *Musique et informatique: bibliographie indexée.* Ivry-sur-Seine: Elmeratto, 1978. 178 pp.

Compilation to mid-1975 on uses of computers in music-making, instruction, acoustics, musicology, music analysis, and music printing, with keywords indicating general topics.

68. Bauer-Mengelberg, Stefan; and Melvin Ferentz. "On eleven-interval twelve-tone rows." *Perspectives of New Music* 3, 2 (spring/summer 1965), 93-103.

Mathematical manipulations of tone rows for use in composition, by means of the computer. A list of interval row generators is given.

69. Bauknight, J. See Metzge and Bauknight.

70. Bayer, Douglas. "Real-time software for a digital music synthesizer." *Computer Music Journal* 1, 4 (Nov. 1977), 22-23.

Description of software for the Alles-DiGiugno synthesizer to control data input from floppy disc memory, to control envelope generation, and to provide for real-time data input.

71. Bearson, James. "Music by computer-- the sound of the future?" *Random Bits* 4, 3 (Nov. 1968), 3-4, 6.

72. Beauchamp, James W. "Additive synthesis of harmonic musical tones." *Journal of the Audio Engineering Society* 14, 4 (Oct. 1966), 332-342.

A solid-state additive synthesis device constructed by the author and called the Harmonic Tone Generator is described. The idea of additive synthesis applied here was subsequently used in digital applications by the author.

73. _____. "Analysis and synthesis of cornet tones using nonlinear interharmonic relationships." *Journal of the Audio Engineering Society* 23, 10 (Dec. 1975), 778-795.

Cornet tones are synthesized digitally by using the first-harmonic envelope to generate several other harmonics in an approximation of the nonlinear interdependence of partials in actual cornet tones. Graphs, diagrams, and charts included.

74. _____. "A computer system for time-variant harmonic analysis and synthesis of musical tones." in *Music by Computers*, ed. by H. von Foerster and J.W. Beauchamp. New York: Wiley and Sons, 1969. 19-62.

Also printed in University of Illinois Experimental Music Studio Technical Report No. 15, Urbana, Aug. 1967. 63 pp.

Research by the author at the University of Illinois involving the use of the Fourier series, modified for time-variant signals, in analysis and synthesis of musical instrument tones is reported. The system involved the use of the Illiac II, IBM 7094, CDC 1604, and CSX-1 computers. Programs for analysis and display, synthesis, and D/A conversion were written by James Fornango and Gary Grossman. Some preliminary conclusions and recorded examples are offered.

75. _____. Electronic instrumentation for synthesis, control, and analysis of harmonic musical tones. Diss., University of Illinois, 1965. 14 pp. *UM* 66-4138. *Dissertation Abstracts* 26 (1965-66), 7213.

Description of the author's Harmonic Tone Generator. This lays the groundwork for digital synthesis of instrumental tones.

76. _____. "Electronic music equipment, 1950-70." University of Illinois Experimental Music Studio Technical Report No. 21, Urbana, Feb. 1970.

77. _____. "An introductory catalogue of computer synthesized sounds." *Perspectives of New Music* 9, 2/10, 1 (Fall-Winter 1971), 348-350.

Review of J.-C. Risset's *Introductory Catalogue of Computer Synthesized Sounds*. See Risset.

78. _____. "Preface." in *Music by Computers*, ed. by H. von Foerster and J.W. Beauchamp. New York: Wiley and Sons, 1969. xi-xv.

79. _____. A report on the Magnavox sponsored investigation 'The development of new electronic systems for generating sounds.' University of Illinois Experimental Music Studio Technical Report No. 10, Urbana, Aug. 1964. 37 pp.

Along with information concerning the activities of the University of Illinois Experimental Music Center during 1963, techniques of sound generation with the CSX-1 and IBM 7090 computers are described.

80. _____. See Foerster and Beauchamp.

81. _____. See Hiller and Beauchamp.

82. _____; and James Fornango. "Transient analysis of musical tones with digital filters." *Journal of the Audio Engineering Society* 15, 1 (1967), 96.

A computer analysis system employing a "hetrodyne filter" is described. The time behaviors of spectral component amplitudes and phases are measured. Design of digital filters for analysis of transients is discussed.

83. _____; and G.R. Grossman. A provisional sound generation program for the Illiac II computer and D/A converter. University of Illinois Experimental Music Studio Technical Report No. 14, Urbana, Sept. 1968.

84. _____; _____; A.B. Otis; and J.A. Cuomo. Four sound processing programs for the Illiac II computer and D/A converter. University of Illinois Experimental Music Studio Technical Report No. 14, Urbana, Sept. 1968.

85. _____; and John Melby. *Composition with Computers*, Proceedings of the Second Annual Music Computation Conference, Nov. 7-9, 1975, part 2. Urbana: University of Illinois, 1975. 83 pp.

Papers by Beckwith, Chadabe, Gressel, Howe, Rothenberg, and Tipei. See separate entries.

86. _____; _____. *Hardware for Computer-Controlled Sound Synthesis,* Proceedings of the Second Annual Music Computation Conference, Nov. 7-9, 1975, part 3. Urbana: University of Illinois, 1975. 59 pp.

Papers by Beauchamp, Pohlman, and Chapman; Gross; Kriz; and Roy. See separate entries.

87. _____; _____. *Information Processing Systems,* Proceedings of the Second Annual Music Computation Conference, Nov. 7-9, 1975, part 4. Urbana: University of Illinois, 1975. 96 pp.

Paper by Austin and Bryant; Charnasse; Dal Molin; Rosenboom; Peters. See Austin and Rosenboom.

88. _____; _____. *Software Synthesis Techniques,* Proceedings of the Second Annual Music Computation Conference, Nov. 7-9, 1975, part 1. Urbana: University of Illinois, 1975. 75 pp.

Papers by Ferretti, Justice, Petersen, Saunders, Kaehler, Zuckerman, Steiglitz, Lake and Cherubini. See separate entries.

89. _____; Ken Pohlman; and Lee Chapman. Modular addressing of a computer controlled synthesizer. Paper presented to the 54th convention of the Audio Engineering Society, Los Angeles, May 4-7, 1976.

A system including a TI980A minicomputer interfaced with a synthesizer is described. The software is designed to create sets of data "triples" which specify action time, device address, and parameter value.

90. _____; _____; _____. "The TI980A
    computer-controlled music synthesizer." In
    *Hardware for Computer-Controlled Sound Syn-
    thesis,* Proceedings of the Second Annual
    Music Computation Conference, Nov. 7-9, 1975,
    part 3. Urbana: University of Illinois, 1975.
    1-36.

    Detailed description of same device present-
    ed above, designed by the authors at the
    University of Illinois. The synthesizer
    employs a modular approach, with a digital
    oscillator for each of four 'voices,' expand-
    able to sixteen.

91. Beckwith, Sterling. "Composing computers for kids--
    a progress report." *Les Cahiers Canadiens
    de Musique/Canada Music Book* 9 (Fall-Winter
    1974), 149-154.

    Description is given of a system which allows
    children or adults to conduct simple experi-
    ments in composition. These are played back
    on five small speakers by the terminal.

92. _____. *The Interactive Music Project at York
    University.* Toronto, Canada: Ontario Ministry
    of Education, 1975.

    Detailed report on the project at York Uni-
    versity for youngsters and adults to learn
    about composition through a digital "sketch-
    pad."

93. _____. "Is a computer 'composing instrument'
    possible?" In *Composition with Computers,*
    Proceedings of the Second Annual Music Comp-
    utation Conference, Nov. 7-9, 1975, part 2.
    Urbana: University of Illinois, 1975. 1-6.

Description of the LOGO digital music
system originally developed at the
Massachussetts Institute of Technology
for children and in operation at York
University. The aims of the project for
creative musical activities and lessons
are outlined.

94. Beigel, Michael. A digital 'phase shifter' for
musical applications, using the Bell
Laboratories (Alles-Fischer) digital
filter module. Paper presented to the
61st convention of the Audio Engineering
Society, New York, Nov. 3-6, 1978.

The operation of the Bell Laboratories
programmable digital filter bank and its
use in simulating a swept analog phase
shifter is described.

95. Behrman, David. "Cell with melody driven electronics
for David Gibson." In *Pieces 3*, ed. by
Michael Byron. Downview, Ont.: York
University and Michael Byron, 1977.

A microprocessor is used with tone generators
tuned in mean-tone temperament, in combination with the 'cello part.

96. Bennett, Gerald. Research at IRCAM in 1977.
Centre Georges Pompidou Rapports IRCAM
No. 1, Paris, 1978.

The first research projects undertaken at
IRCAM (Institut de Recherche et Coordination
Acoustique/Musique) include digital synthesis
with general-purpose computers, digital synthesis with specific devices, and psychoacoustic studies to aid synthesis, and are
summarized here.

97. _____. see Mathews and Bennett.

98. Bense, Max. "Kunst aus dem Computer." *Exakte Ästhetik 5, Methoden in Ergibniss empirischer und experimenteller Ästhetik.* Stuttgart, 1957.

Conclusions of the author pertaining to aesthetic considerations in the use of computers in art and music.

99. Berlind, Gary. "Writings on the use of computers in music." *College Music Symposium* 6 (Fall 1966), 143-157.

A later version appears in *Musicology and the Computer,* ed. Barry S. Brook. New York: City University of New York Press, 1970. 229-270.

100. Bernfeld, Benjamin; and Bennet Smith. Computer-aided model of stereophonic systems. Centre Georges Pompidou Rapports IRCAM No. 15, Paris, 1978.

The model is intended to simulate the stereophonic localization response and other important characteristics of reproduced sound. This project, carried out at the Institut de Recherche et Coordination Acoustique/Musique, may find eventual application in digital sound synthesis.

101. Bernstein, Alan D.; and Ellis D. Cooper. "The piecewise linear technique of electronic music synthesis." *Journal of the Audio Engineering Society* 24, 6 (July/Aug. 1976), 446-454.

A new generator permitting direct analog control of acoustic waveforms ('piecewise linear generator') has been developed. A

23

FORTRAN program, facilitating the computation of amplitude spectra, is used in discussing the properties of the module. Various applications are suggested.

102. Binkley, Thomas E. "Electronic processing of musical materials." in *Elektronische Datenverarbeitung in der Musikwissenschaft,* ed. by Harald Heckmann. Regensburg: Gustav Bosse, 1967. 1-20.

103. Bischoff, John; Rich Gold; and Jim Horton. "Music for an interactive network of microcomputers." *Computer Music Journal* 2, 3 (Dec. 1978), 24-29.

Description of performance given by the authors at the Blind Lemon, a gallery in Berkeley, California, July 3, 1978. A system of three microcomputers (KIM-1) was used, connected in a circular arrangement, with two outputs of direct D/A conversion.

104. Blesser, Barry A. Digital processing of audio signals. Paper presented at the Midwest Acoustics Conference, Evanston, Illinois, April 5, 1975.

Analog-to-digital and digital-to-analog converters, and characteristics of sampled data systems are discussed. Many applications of these principles, including music generation, are discussed.

105. Bodin, Lars-Gunnar. "Mobilis in mobile." *Nutida Musik* 16, 2 (1972-73), 29-30.

Introduction to the use of computers in composition.

106. _____. "Samtal med Alan Sutcliffe och
     Jonathon Harvey." *Nutida Musik* 16, 2
     (1972-73), 33-36.

     Interview with Alan Sutcliffe, president of
     the Computer Arts Society, and with Jonathon
     Harvey. The Computer Arts Society is an organ-
     ization for people interested in the creative
     use of computers for artistic purposes.

107. Bois, Mario. *Iannis Xenakis, the man and his
     music; a conversation with the composer and
     a description of his works.* London: Boosey
     and Hawkes, 1967. 40 pp.

     Translation of "Xenakis, musicien d'avant-garde."
     Bulletin d'Information Boosey and Hawkes 23
     (Sept. 1966), 2-22.

     A biography, chronological list of Xenakis'
     works to date, a bibliography of writings by
     and about Xenakis, a discography, interview,
     and comments on the composer's work by various
     associates are all included.

108. Borko, Harold, ed. *Computer Applications in the
     Behavioral Sciences.* Englewood Cliffs, N.J.:
     Prentice-Hall, 1962. 633 pp.

     Includes article by L. Hiller and R. Baker,
     "Computer music."

109. Bourgeois, Jacques. *Iannis Xenakis, entretien
     avec Jacques Bourgeois.* Paris: Boosey and
     Hawkes, 1970. 40 pp.

     Interview with the composer. Illustrated
     coverage of a radio broadcast by France-
     culture, in October 1968.

110. Boudinot, R.D. "Development of a standard orchestra for computer-generated sound." *Computers and the Humanities* 6, 2 (Nov. 1971), 123.

Report on the author's work in progress on an orchestra compiler for the MUSIC V program developed at Bell Laboratories.

111. _____. Development of INSGEN: an orchestra compiler for computer-generated sound. Diss., University of Miami, 1972. *Dissertation Abstracts* 34, 10 (1974), 6681A.

An instrument generating compiler has been written to be added to a MUSIC V sound generating program. The compiler also accepts data from an A/D converter.

112. Brainerd, Robert F. Two musical applications of computer programming. National Science Foundation Project No. GK-14191 Technical Report No. 3, Buffalo, N.Y., 1972. 125 pp.

Includes article by Hiller and Ruiz, "Synthesizing musical sounds by solving the wave equation for vibrating objects."

113. Brickle, Frank. "Music Computation Conference II." *Contemporary Music Newsletter* 9, 5 (1975), 1-2.

Review of conference held at the University of Illinois, Nov. 7-9, 1975.

114. Bromose, Ole. *Beskrivelse af programmet SIM.* Aarhus: Institute of Musicology, Department of Musical Acoustics, 1975.

Users' manual for the EGG synthesizer constructed at the University of Aarhus.

115. _____. SIM-projektets status pr 1/9 1974.
unpublished manuscript, Aarhus, 1974.

116. _____. Simulering af en 200 UT. Unpublished
manuscript, Aarhus, n.d.

117. _____; and Finn Egeland Hansen. "A survey
of the SIM system, a computer system for
performing acoustical analysis and synthesis."
Electronic Music and Musical Acoustics
[Aarhus: University of Aarhus Institute of
Musicology] 1 (1975), 45.

   Description is given of a system which makes
   use of a CDC 6400 computer and local TI 960A
   minicomputer. A/D and D/A conversion, digital
   waveform generation programs are written in
   PASCAL. Two printed outputs from the system
   are given as examples.

118. Brooks, F.P.; A.L. Hopkins, Jr.; P. Newman; and
W.V. Wright. "An experiment in musical
composition." *Institute of Radio Engineers
Transactions on Electronic Computers* EC-6, 3
(Sept. 1957), 175-182.

   Original melodies were synthesized by a
   random process, using tables derived from
   a probabilistic analysis of hymn tunes.
   Included in this article are comparative
   statistics of syntheses using eight orders
   of analysis and notated examples of the
   melodies produced. A correction to this
   article appears in *IRE Transactions on
   Electronic Computers* EC-7 (1958), 60.

119. Brün, Herbert. "Composition with computers." In
Cybernetic Serendipity, ed. Jasia Reichardt.
New York: Praeger, 1969. 20.

Brün, continued

120. _____. "Ersättning eller Analogie: Datama-
skinmusikestetik." *Nutida Musik* 9, 7 (1965-
1966), 27-31.

Reflections on aesthetic considerations in
the use of computers in composition.

121. _____. "From musical ideas to computers and
back." In *The Computer and Music*, ed. by
Harry B. Lincoln. Ithaca: Cornell University
Press, 1970. 23-36.

Discussion of attitudes and musical ideas
that lead a composer to make use of the computer, and the new musical systems one might
derive from such activity.

122. _____. "*Infraudibles*." In *Music by Computers*,
ed. by H. von Foerster and J.W. Beauchamp.
New York: Wiley and Sons, 1969. 117-121.

The composer discusses the musical ideas of
his *Infraudibles*, a computer-generated composition, and the general aesthetic significance of the use of computers in composition.
A recording of the work is included.

123. _____. "Mutatis Mutandis." *Numus West* [Mer-
cer Island, Wash.] 4 (1973), 31-34.

Also appears as "Mutatis Mutandis: compositions pour interprètes." *Les Cahiers Sesa*
5 (1973), 22-23.

Ink graphics drawn with the aid of the IBM
7094 computer and Calcomp plotter are reproduced here. These works are intended as images of the mental process of composition
and as bases for further artistic activity.

124. _____. "Research on the conditions under which a system of computers would assist a composer in creating works of a contemporary relevance and significance." *Proceedings of the First Meeting of the American Society of University Composers*. Princeton: Princeton University, 1966. 30-37.

The relationship between artificial systems and the necessary organization of the composer's mind is explored, with the conclusion being that the self-imposed restrictions that composers must always choose may be transferred to the computer system.

125. _____. "*Sawdust*." (Available through Lingua Press). In *Lingua Press Collection Two Catalogue*. La Jolla, Calif.: Lingua Press, 1978. N.pag.

Presentation of H. Brün's project *Sawdust*, a two-channel stereo tape of two pieces produced with the aid of the computer, *Dust, op. 45*, and *More Dust, op. 46*.

126. _____. "Technology and the composer." in *Music and Technology*. Paris: La Revue Musicale, 1971. 181-92.

Also, as "La technologie et le compositeur." *La Revue Musicale* 268-269 (1971), 181-193.

A composer's views on computers, technology in general, and the role in the arts and in society that they may play.

127. _____. ". . . to hold discourse, at least with a computer." *Guildhall School of Music and Drama Review* [London], 1973. 16-21.

128. _____. *Über Musik und zum Computer.*
Karlsruhe: G. Braun Verlag, 1971. 129 pp.

Twenty of the "Mutatis Mutandis" graphics
by the author; essays on music, art, and
technology; scores from computer-generated
sound compositions; and a recording are included.

129. Bryant, Larry. See Austin and Bryant.

130. Buchla, Don; and Richard Friedman. A computer
aided analog electronic music system. Paper
presented to the 42nd convention of the Audio
Engineering Society, Los Angeles, May 2-5,
1972.

Description of a system which uses a small
computer to input, display, store, and recall
complex patching networks, in conjunction
with analog hardware.

131. Budzynski, Gustav; Marianna Sankiewicz. "Komput-
er analogowy w muzyce eksperymentalneż."
*Zeszyty Naukowe. Państwowa Wyższa Szkoła
Muzyczna* [Poland] 12 (1973), 107-120. Mimeo.

Description of the application of computers
in composing music and the practical use of
smaller computers in the experimental music
studio. A list of works is included.

132. Bukharaev, R. G.; and M. S. Rytvinsskaya. "Simulating a probabilistic process connected
with composing a melody." *Kazan Universitet
Uchenye Zapiske* 122, 4 (1962), 82-97.

Production of tunes making use of a random
number generator and stored rules of composition which are imposed on random selection.

133. Burhans, R. W. "Digital tone synthesis." *Journal of the Audio Engineering Society* 19, 8 (Sept. 1971), 660-663.

Digital logic circuits are used to generate a three-octave equal-tempered scale, with the aim of producing a low-cost keyboard controlled synthesizer. The tone generator operates on the principle of digital frequency division, and produces square waves. The method largely eliminates tuning problems found in other synthesizers.

134. _____. "Single-bus keyboard control for digital musical instruments." *Journal of the Audio Engineering Society* 19, 10 (Nov. 1971), 865.

A type of switch simplifying keyboard hardware for digital synthesizers is described.

135. Buxton, William S. "A composer's introduction to computer music." *Interface* 6, 2 (Sept. 1977), 57-72.

Revision of "Computers and the composer: an introductory survey." *Faire* [Bourges: Editions GMEB] 4/5 (1975).

A historical survey of computer music is presented, including approaches to both computer composition and sound synthesis techniques (digital and hybrid). Bibliography.

136. _____, ed. *Computer Music 1976/77: a directory to current work.* Ottawa, Ont.: Canadian Commission for UNESCO, 1977. 239 pp.

Eighty studios in fifteen countries are listed, with information on the facilities, staff, funding, projects in progress, compositions completed, and instruction offered. Studios listed were all respondants to a questionnaire.

137. _____. *Manual for the POD Programs.* Utrecht: Institute of Sonology, University of Utrecht, 1974.

Users' manual for programs developed by Barry Truax at the Institute of Sonology, which make use of J. Chowning's FM technique of digital synthesis and also probabilistic methods of composition.

138. _____. "Recherches effectuées à Utrecht." *Faire* [Bourges: Editions GMEB] 2-3 (1975), 101-102.

139. _____. See Federkow, Buxton, and Smith.

140. _____; E.A. Fogels; Guy Federkow; Lawrence Sasaki; and K.C. Smith. "An introduction to the SSSP digital synthesizer." *Computer Music Journal* 2, 4 (late Dec. 1978), 28-38.

General architecture and design details of a digital synthesizer developed at the University of Toronto are presented. This system incorporates five techniques of sound synthesis: fixed waveform, frequency modulation, additive synthesis, waveshaping, and pulse width modulation (after the VOSIM oscillator of S. Tempelaars). References included.

141. _____; and Paul Pignon. "Systems en temps réel et interaction homme-machine." *Faire* [Bourges: Editions GMEB] 2-3 (1975), 185-186.

142. _____; William Reeves; Ronald Baecker; and
Leslie Mezer. "The use of hierarchy and
instance in a data structure for computer
music." *Computer Music Journal* 2, 4
(late Dec. 1978), 10-20.

The music system of the Structured Sound
Synthesis Project at the University of
Toronto is described. Flowcharts are included,
and each of four types of data structure
(scores, sound objects, functions, waveforms)
are described in terms of internal representation and links between files. Bibliography
included.

143. Byrd, Donald. "Humanities programming for creative work." *Random Bits* 6, 5 (Jan. 1971),
8-12.

144. _____. "An integrated computer music software system." *Computer Music Journal* 1, 2
(April 1977), 55-60.

Computer music software at Indiana University
is described. Programs are batch-oriented and
integrated so that data from one program can
be passed to another, through interface programs and translators. The programs include
Xenakis' free stochastic music program, a
program by Byrd for converting MUSIC V cards
to conventional music notation for a music
printing program; a music input encoding
language by J. Wenker; analysis programs by
Wenker and D. Gross; MUSIC V for sound synthesis; utility programs by G. Cohn; twelve-
tone composing program by Byrd; and a sound-
synthesis language compiler by Cohn. Additional
programs (organ keyboard and tablet programs)
may be run on another system (Xerox Sigma 5)
to generate data for the larger system.

145. Cann, R.; P. Lansky; K. Steiglitz; and
     M. Zuckerman. Practical considerations in
     the application of linear prediction to music
     synthesis. Paper presented at the First
     International Conference on Computer Music,
     Massachussetts Institute of Technology, Oct.
     28-31, 1976.

     The method of linear prediction is outlined,
     and the programs required for the analysis
     of speech, using this method, are described.
     Problems of resynthesis of speech and solu-
     tions to problems which arise in a MUSIC IV
     system are presented.

146. Castman, Bernt. "Musik och computer." *Svensktid-
     skrift för musikforskning* 52 (1970), 46-50.

     Discussion of computer applications in re-
     search and composition (including hybrid sys-
     tems, digital synthesis, and data transcribed
     from print-outs to common musical notation).
     Plans are presented for the use of a computer
     in the Elektronmusikstudion in Stockholm.

147. Caussé, René. Unite électronique destinée à la
     transformation du son en temps réel, program-
     mable et controlable par l'instrumentiste.
     Centre Georges Pompidou Rapports IRCAM No. 2,
     1978.

     A small analog electronic filter/modulator
     device with changeable interconnection matrix
     was used in the work *KOEXISTENZ* for two 'celli,
     one unmodified and the other modified and
     amplified. Technical description and circuit
     diagrams are given, as well as a description
     of the rehearsals of the work.

148. Ceely, Robert P. A composer's view of MITSYN.
     Paper presented to the 41st convention of
     the Audio Engineering Society, New York,
     Oct. 5-8, 1971. Preprint No. 811.

     Presentation on a project called Musical
     Interactive Tone Synthesis, a system design-
     ed for composition, with emphasis on control
     of timbre. The programming of this digital
     system allows the composer to approach the
     system in much the same way as an electronic
     synthesizer.

149. Chadabe, Joel. "Das elektronische Studio von
     Albany." *Melos* 33, 5 (May 1971), 188-190.

     A hybrid digital-analog system developed by
     the author and constructed by Robert Moog at
     the State University of New York at Albany
     is described.

150. _____. "Some reflections on the nature of the
     landscape within which computer music systems
     are designed." *Computer Music Journal* 1, 3
     (June 1977), 5-11.

     General considerations in computer music sys-
     tem design and use of programming sub-systems
     are discussed. Comments are made on C. Dodge's
     Earth's Magnetic Field, Max Mathew's Conduct-
     or Program and MUSIC V system, L. Hiller's
     Illiac Suite, the author's own *Echoes,*
     S. Martirano's SalMar Construction, and
     D. Buchla's Series 500 Electric Music Box.

151. _____. "System composing." In *Composition
     with Computers,* Proceedings of the Second
     Annual Music Computation Conference, Nov. 7-9,
     1975, part 2. Urbana: University of Illinois,
     1975. 7-10.

Concepts taken from systems philosophy are seen to provide a basis for change in music newly composed, along with technological tools such as computers. The idea of composition as the creation of a system is explicated.

152. _____; and Roger Meyers. "An introduction to the PLAY program." *Computer Music Journal* 2, 1 (July 1978), 12-18.

A program called PLAY, written at the electronic music studio at the State University of New York in Albany, is described. The program is designed to allow the composer maximum choice of temporal processes, real-time interaction, and is to be used with a small computer controlling an external synthesizer (analog or digital), or possibly a video synthesizer. PLAY was first presented at the Computer Music Conference at San Diego, Cal., in Oct. 1977, with the name RTMS1.

153. Chamberlain, Howard W. "Experimental Fourier series universal tone generator." *Journal of the Audio Engineering Society* 24, 4 (May 1976), 271-276.

Also, presented at the 51st convention of the Audio Engineering Society, Los Angeles, May 13-16, 1975. Preprint No. 1023.

A digital instrument capable of real-time computation of a 32-term Fourier series is described. Amplitude and phase of each harmonic are variable. Other features include techniques for realizing inexact harmonic frequencies, simulating fixed or variable filters, and synthesizing multiple tones.

154. Chamberlin, Hal. "A sampling of techniques for the computer performance of music." *Byte* 2, 9 (Sept. 1977), 62.

A brief history of digital sound-generation and an explanation of the sampling theorem, various terms, and basic ideas are present- ed. Addressing himself to computer hobbyists, the author suggests that earlier techniques be adapted for smaller computers and de- scribes his own language, NOTRAN, for con- verting musical terms to physical units of measure.

155. Champernowne, P.G. Music from EDSAC. Cambridge University Technical Report, Cambridge, England, 1961.

A computer program which produces data for transcription into musical notation is de- tailed here. Music for a string quartet was produced from the program.

156. Chang, Jih-Jie; and Max V. Mathews. Program for automatically plotting the scores of comput- er sound sequences. Murray Hill, N.J.: Bell Laboratories, n.d. Mimeo.

157. _____; _____. "Score-drawing program." *Journal of the Audio Engineering Society* 15, 3 (July 1967), 279-281.

Description of a computer program used with available microfilm plotting equipment for automatic plotting of graphical scores of computer-generated sound sequences. A sample of the graphical score is included.

158. Chapman, Lee. See Beauchamp, Pohlman, and Chapman.

159. Charbonneau, Gérard. "L'ordinateur, instrument
     de musique: synthèse directe des sons."
     *Conférences des Journées d'Etudes, Festival
     International du Son.* Paris: Ed. Radio,
     1973.

     Introduction to sound synthesis at larger
     computer installations. Illustrations
     included.

160. _____. See Risset, Charbonneau, and
     Karantchentzeff.

161. Charles, Daniel. *La Pensée de Xenakis.* Paris:
     Boosey and Hawkes, n.d.

162. Charnassé, Hélène. "L'informatique musicale en
     1974." *Journal de la Societé de Statistique
     de Paris* 115, 3 (1974), 210-215.

     Survey of computer music activities to date.

163. Chernoff, Lionel. The determination of all
     possible hexachord-generated twelve-tone
     rows characterized by bisymmetric configura-
     tions of all simple intervals. Diss.,
     Catholic University, 1968. 79 pp. *UM*69-9092.
     Dissertation Abstracts 30 (1969-70), 354A.

164. Cherubini, Ralph. See Lake and Cherubini.

165. Chion, Michel; and Bénédict Maillard, eds.
     *Cahiers recherche/musique: synthétiseur
     ordinateur* [Paris: Institut National de
     l'Audio-visuel et Groupe de Recherches
     Musicales] 1, 3 (1976), 1-278.

     Entire issue devoted to computer use in
     sound synthesis, including articles by
     Dürr, Jaffrennou, Allouis, and Maillard.
     See separate entries.

166. Choate, Robert A. "Impact and potentials of tech-
     nology." *Documentary Report of the Tanglewood
     Symposium*. Washington: Music Educators'
     National Conference, 1968. 123-126.

167. Chong, John. *Computer and Electronic Music in
     Europe-- 1973*. Ottawa, Ont.: National Research
     Council of Canada, 1974. 48 pp.

     Survey including activities in Utrecht, Ghent,
     Cologne, Plzen and Bratislava in Czechoslovakia,
     in Paris by the Groupe de Recherches Musicales,
     and in London at the Electronic Music Studio, Ltd.

168. _____. "The studio in London." In *Musical
     Aspects of the Electronic Medium*, Report on
     Electronic Music, ed. F. Weiland. Utrecht:
     Institute of Sonology, 1975.

     Descriptions of the facilities and on-going
     activities at the Electronic Music Studio
     London, Ltd., founded by P. Zinovieff, are
     given. A list of completed works is included.

169. Chowning, John. Conceptual model for the genera-
     tion of string tones. Presented to the IRCAM
     Symposium on Musical and Psycho-acoustics,
     Paris, 1977.

170. _____. "The simulation of moving sound sources."
     Journal of the Audio Engineering Society 19, 1
     (Jan. 1971), 2-6.

     Reprinted in *Computer Music Journal* 1, 3
     (June 1977), 48-52.

     A technical description of the use of a digital
     computer to generate four-channel sound with
     programmed control of location is given here.
     Location and movement are simulated by control
     of distribution of sound between channels,
     amplitude of direct and reverberant signals,

and Doppler shift, providing the effect of direction, distance, and velocity perception.

171. _____. "Stanford Computer Music Project." *Numus-West* [Mercer Island, Washington] 1 (1972), 12-14.

Portions of this report reprinted from the *Journal of the Audio Engineering Society* 19, 1 (Jan. 1971), 2-6.

Description of on-going research at the Stanford University Computer Music Project, specifically the author's own work on the simulation of sound sources moving through space, using digital sound synthesis.

172. _____. "The synthesis of complex audio spectra by means of frequency modulation." *Journal of the Audio Engineering Society* 21, 7 (Sept. 1973), 526-534.

Also, presented at the 46th convention of the Audio Engineering Society, New York, Sept. 10-13, 1973.
Reprinted in *Computer Music Journal* 1, 2 (April 1977), 46.
Reprinted in *Musical Aspects of the Electronic Medium*, Report on Electronic Music, ed. F. Weiland. Utrecht: Institute of Sonology, 1975.

Classic article on a technique developed by the author which produces a great variety of rich timbres by a means simpler than additive or subtractive synthesis. This idea has inspired many applications involving smaller computers. A detailed technical description is given, with diagrams, graphs, and techniques for simulating musical instrument tones using frequency modulation.

173. _____. See Smith and Chowning.

174. _____; J. Grey; J.A. Moorer; and L. Rush.
Computer simulation of music instrument tones
in reverberant environments. Stanford University Department of Music Technical Report
STAN-M-1, Stanford, Calif., July 1974.

Reprint of portions of a National Science
Foundation proposal which resulted in a grant
to the computer music group at Stanford. The
main area of inquiry described here is the
simulation of music instrument tones in reverberant spaces.

175. Christiansen, Steven. "A microprocessor-controlled
digital waveform generator." *Journal of the
Audio Engineering Society* 25, 5 (May 1977),
299-309.

Also, presented to the 54th convention of the
Audio Engineering Society, Los Angeles, May 4-7,
1976.

A system utilizing a MOS Technology 6502
microprocessor and a digital waveform generator
based on the sine-wave generation algorithm
developed by Kaegi and Tempelaars at the University of Utrecht (their VOSIM system) is
described. Preliminary work and future plans
for the project at Iowa State University are
discussed. Programs and print-outs are included.

176. Ciamaga, Gustav. "The training of the composer in
new technological means." In *Music and Technology*. Paris: La Revue Musicale, 1971. 143-150.

Also, as "Initiation du compositeur aux
nouveaux procédés technologiques." *La Revue
Musicale* 268-269 (1971), 139-147.

The author proposes a training plan for young

41

composers in the use of technological aides, including the computer, in modern composition.

177. _____. See Gabura and Ciamaga.

178. Clark, H.D. New electronic music studio in Norway. Paper presented to the 50th convention of the Audio Engineering Society, London, March 4-7, 1975. Included in the *Collected Preprints of the 50th Audio Engineering Society Convention*. London: AES, 1975.

The studio described ("Electric Music Box 502") includes analog components, a polyphonic keyboard, and a desk-top computer.

179. Clark, Melville. See Strong and Clark.

180. Clark, Robert K. MAESTRO-- A program for the real-time generation of musical sounds. Argonne National Laboratories Technical Memorandum No. 106, Sept. 1975.

Reprinted as "A program for the real-time generation of musical sounds." *Journal of the Audio Engineering Society* 14, 1 (1966), 21-29.
Also, presented at the 17th convention of the Audio Engineering Society, New York, Oct. 11-15, 1965.

A technical description from the user's point of view is given for the program MAESTRO, written for a small computer (the ASI-210). Clock-rate is 6000 interrupts/sec. Flow-charts, tables of program functions, graphs, and a print-out are included.

181. Clough, John. "Computer music and group theory." *Proceedings of the American Society of University Composers* 4 (April 1969), 10-19.

Fundamentals of the mathematical theory of groups are presented and applied to existing programs for sound generation.

182. _____. "Computer sound-generation: an educational resource at Oberlin College." *Proceedings of a Conference on Computers in the Undergraduate Curricula: June 1970.* Iowa City, Ia.: Center for Conferences and Institutes, 1970. 1.18-1.19.

A set of three courses with separate analog and digital facilities for electronic sound-generation are available to undergraduate students at Oberlin College, and are described here.

183. _____. "An interactive system for computer sound generation." *Proceedings of the American Society of University Composers* 6 (1971), 22-26.

System developed at Oberlin College, called IRMA, is described. Features of "human intervention" for modification of programmed material in various ways are explained.

184. _____. "IRMA: an interactive, real-time system for electronic music." *IEEE* [Institute of Electronic and Electrical Engineers] *International Convention Digest,* March 1971, 4-41.

IRMA (Interactive Real-time Music Assembler), a digital system developed at Oberlin College in 1969-70, is described. This system has a digital loop which is converted to analog form and monitored by the composer. The loop may be modified by an on-line device, changing the data while the loop is being converted, with immediate results.

Clough, continued

185. _____. "A report from Oberlin." *Computer Music Newsletter* 1, 1 (Feb. 1971), 2-5.

Computer sound-generation at Oberlin College is described, including the hardware configuration, the digital-to-analog converter, the TEMPO language, the IRMA system, and the educational program in electronic music there.

186. _____. "TEMPO: A composer's programming language." *Perspectives of New Music* 9, 1 (fall-winter 1970), 113-125.

A general description of TEMPO (Transformational Electronic Music Process Organizer), designed by the author and Eric Sosman. Its special features are enumerated, with emphasis on the automatic generation of a score.

187. Cohen, David. User's manual for PERFORM. Arizona State University, 1968. Ms.

188. _____. "Yet another sound generation program." *Proceedings of the American Society of University Composers* 4 (April 1969), 20-22.

Description of a simplified version of the programs developed at Bell Laboratories, in FORTRAN, called PERFORM. The aim was to design a program that is easy for the uninitiated to learn to use.

189. Cohen, Joel E. "Information theory and music." *Behavioral Science* 7 (1962), 137-163.

The technical and aesthetic assumptions made in previous applications of information theory to music, results obtained, and a critique are presented. The idea of music as a

Markov chain, styles as probability systems, and statistical analyses of musical works are evaluated. Bibliography included.

190. Cohn, George. SOUND language. Paper presented at the First International Conference on Computer Music, Massachussetts Institute of Technology, Oct. 28-31, 1976.

SOUND is a procedure-oriented language for writing digital sound synthesis programs, which attempts to accommodate any conceivable conceptual framework. It is implemented on a CDC 6600 system. Event generators (composition routines) and sample generators ("instruments") of the language are discussed in some detail.

191. _____. Users' manual for SOUND. Unpublished manuscript. Wrubel Computing Center, Indiana University.

192. "College Music Society: report of the eighth annual meeting, second session." *College Music Symposium* 6 (Fall 1966), 124-133.

Summaries of papers presented by Leo S. Packer, Barry S. Brook, and A. Wayne Slawson.

193. Computer Arts Society. *Page: bulletin of the Computer Arts Society* [Pergamon Press, U.K.]. 1969- .

Newsletter of the Computer Arts Society, whose chairman is Alan Sutcliffe. It appears eight times yearly, with one of these issues being edited in the U.S. by Kurt Lauckner. Articles on the use of computers for artistic purposes of all sorts are included.

194. Computer Faire. *Proceedings of the First West Coast Computer Faire*. Palo Alto, Calif.: Computer Faire, 1977. 300 pp.

   A conference on personal and home computers was held in April 1977, in San Francisco. Topics included music and computers and computer art systems. Papers plus names and addresses of exhibitors are given here.

195. Conly, Paul; and Allen Radzow. Digital composition and control of an electronic music synthesizer. Paper presented at the 41st convention of the Audio Engineering Society, New York, Oct. 5-8, 1971.

   A hybrid system with software (COMPOSER III) which produces sound via digital synthesis or through the synthesizer interface is described. Algorithms for probabilistic controls of random elements introduced into composition are provided.

196. Cooper, Ellis D. See Bernstein and Cooper.

197. Cooper, James. A hybrid microcomputer voice and music synthesis system. Paper presented to the 58th convention of the Audio Engineering Society, New York, Nov. 4-7, 1977.

   A portable computer system has been built with an interface to voice and music synthesizers. The system can be programmed to perform ensemble music with up to eight voices and four "instruments" in real-time.

198. Coren, Daniel; and Harry Mendell. A mini-computer-based sound manipulation system. Paper presented to the 57th convention of the Audio Engineering Society, Los Angeles, May 10-13, 1977.

The system described features simulation of digital delay systems, multiple-head variable-speed tape machines, and 'harmonizers.' A library of novel reverberant sounds is stored in the computer's memory.

199. Cotton, Robert B., Jr. "Tempered scale generation from a single frequency source." *Journal of the Audio Engineering Society* 20, 5 (June 1972), 376-382.

Also presented to the 41st convention of the Audio Engineering Society, New York, Oct. 5-8, 1971.

A master oscillator in conjunction with a digital calculating system has been developed for tempered scale generation, to be used by the Hammond Organ Company.

200. Cremer, L., ed. *Proceedings of the Third International Congress on Acoustics, Stuttgart, 1959.* In two vols. Amsterdam: Elsevier, 1961. 1320 pp.

Includes article by Mathews and Guttman, "Generation of music by a digital computer," 253-254.

201. Creutz, Thomas. An interactive graphical interface for MIT's MUSIC 360 language for digital sound synthesis. Paper read at the First International Conference on Computer Music, Massachussetts Institute of Technology, Oct. 28-31, 1976.

MUSIC 360/GRAPHIC is a three-step program allowing a user to create a set of graphical forms (block diagram, function, and score) on the screen of an interactive graphics terminal. It is to be used in con-

junction with B. Vercoe's MUSIC 360 program
for sound synthesis.

202. Cross, Lowell. *A Bibliography of Electronic
Music*. Toronto: University of Toronto
Press, 1967. 126 pp.

203. _____. "Electronic music, 1948-1953."
Perspectives of New Music 7, 1 (Fall-Winter
1968), 32-65.

Reprinted in *Musical Aspects of the Electronic
Medium*, Report on Electronic Music, ed. by
Frits Weiland. Utrecht: Institute of Sonology,
1975.

Documentation of early experimentation and
composition in electronic music and with
computers. The information here was derived
from original sources, and this article has
served as source material for many histories
of electronic music written more recently.

204. Crowhurst, Norman H. *Electronic Musical Instruments*. Blue Ridge Summit, Pa.: Tab, 1971.

This compendium of electronic musical instruments also includes a section on the use of
computer programs and punched tape to control synthesizers.

205. Cuomo, J.A. See Beauchamp, Grossman, Otis, and
Cuomo.

206. _____. See Grossman and Cuomo.

207. Danish State Radio. "The idea behind the creation of DRS television interval signal."
Numus West [Mercer Island, Washington] 4

(1973), 42-44.

An application of computer-generated music
is described: intervals between television
programs are filled with "calendar music"
which is altered each day by means of programming changes, methodically varying scale,
tempo, volume, and density, as well as the
correlated visual images.

208. Dausell, Tinne. Samspilformen, traditionelle
instrumenter/elektronisk lyd. Diss., University of Aarhus, 1974.

209. Davis, Bob. "David Rosenboom-- recent cybernetic
insights." *Synapse* 2, 4 (Jan.-Feb. 1978),
18.

Description of Rosenboom's hybrid analog/di-
gital electronic music instrument, which
utilizes an Interdata mini-computer, complex
waveform generators, and a video terminal.
Activities of the Aesthetic Research Center
in Vancouver are also discussed.

210. _____. "Guerilla electronics-- more monkey
business." *Synapse* 1, 5 (Jan.-Feb. 1977),
26-29.

Use of a microprocessor system (Altair 680
featuring Motorola 6800 processor family)
for a voltage-controlled sound-and-light
composition by Bob Gonsalves. The piece was
presented at a concert of the Center for
Contemporary Music, Mills College, Oct. 24,
1976.

211. _____. See Pittman and Davis.

212. Debelius, Ulrich. "Szene und Technik. Zwei Aspekte einer Entwicklung." In *Die Musik der sechziger Jahre*. Regensburg: Gustav Bosse Verlag, 1973. 53-64.

Two dominating trends in music produced during the 1960's are seen: the use of theatrical forces and the synthetic generation of sound by means of computers and electronics. Compositions representing these two trends are examined, including *Eonta* by I. Xenakis, *Function Grün* by G.M. Koenig, and *Infraudibles* by H. Brün.

213. Debiasi, Giovanni. See Poli and Debiasi.

214. DeCrescent, Ron. A computer-based research laboratory for sound-processing and analysis. Paper presented to the 45th convention of the Audio Engineering Society, Los Angeles, May 15-18, 1973.

A facility, primarily designed for speech analysis, which uses a small general-purpose computer for the processing and analysis of sound samples is described.

215. Denes, F.B. See Mathews and Denes.

216. Deutsche, Ralph. Digital system for a realistic organ tone generator. Paper presented to the 41st convention of the Audio Engineering Society, New York, Oct. 5-8, 1971.

A completely digital system for generating pipe organ tones is described. Extensive use is made of time-multiplexing.

217. Deutschman, Ben. "Music from mathematics." *Music Journal* 22, 7 (Oct. 1964), 54-56.

Critique of the recordings produced at Bell Laboratories and released as "Music from Mathematics."

218. DiGiugno, Giuseppe. A real-time computer-controlled oscillator bank. Paper presented at the First International Conference on Computer Music, Massachussetts Institute of Technology, Oct. 28-31, 1976.

A digital oscillator bank of 256 virtual oscillators and four channels of D/A output has been constructed for a large-scale real-time digital synthesizer at IRCAM (Institut de Recherche et Coordination Acoustique/Musique) in Paris. The central feature of the system is a single time-shared table look-up digital oscillator and amplitude modulator.

219. _____; and H.G. Alles. "A one-card 64-channel digital synthesizer." *Computer Music Journal* 1, 4 (Nov. 1977), 7-9.

Also, as Rapports IRCAM No. 4, Centre Georges Pompidou, Paris, 1978. 2 pp.
Also, presented at the 1977 International Computer Music Conference, Center for Music Experiment and Related Research, University of California at San Diego, Oct. 1977.

Description of a digital synthesizer providing 64 oscillators at a 32 Khz. sampling rate, with 128 envelope generators and 15 accumulating and interconnecting registers. This is a one-card special purpose processor intended to be used as part of a larger system, interfaced with DEC's LSI-11 micro-computer. The authors are associated with

the French research center IRCAM and with
Bell Laboratories, respectively.

220. Dimond, Stuart Dudley III. Microprocessor-based
control and generation techniques for electronic music. Paper presented at the 54th
convention of the Audio Engineering Society,
Los Angeles, May 4-7, 1976.

Design of a microprocessor-based interface
with a polyphonic digital synthesizer is described. Application as a keyboard, guitar,
or electronic brass synthesizer is suggested.

221. "Directory of scholars active-- music." *Computers
and the Humanities* 2, 5 (May 1968), 241-245.

222. "Directory of scholars active-- music." *Computers
and the Humanities* 3, 5 (May 1969), 310-312.

223. "Directory of scholars active-- music." *Computers
and the Humanities* 4, 2 (Nov. 1970), 138.

224. "Directory of scholars active-- music." *Computers
and the Humanities* 8, 4 (1974), 254-255.

225. "Directory of scholars active-- music." *Computers
and the Humanities* 9, 1 (1975), 33.

226. "Directory of scholars active-- music." *Computers
and the Humanities* 9, 4 (1975), 192-193.

227. "Directory of scholars active-- music." *Computers
and the Humanities* 10, 1 (1976), 51-52.

228. "Directory of scholars active-- music." *Computers
and the Humanities* 11, 1 (1977), 41-42.

In the articles above, descriptions can be
found of the current work of D. MacInnis,
M. Mathews, G. Strang, E.G. Kobrin, J. Clough,

Leland Smith, J. Chowning, Gary Nelson,
J.-C. Risset, O. Laske, D. Byrd, and others.
Information is given in abbreviated form on
the scope of the project, type of computer
used, language and level used, special equipment, number and type of tapes, and whether
the program is available.

229. Divilbiss, S.I. "The real-time generation of music
with a digital computer." *Journal of Music
Theory* 8 (Spring 1964), 99.

The article begins with a general description
of Mathews' methods at Bell Laboratories,
then presents the author's own system devised
at the Coordinated Science Laboratory at the
University of Illinois. This system involves
the use of a CSX-1 computer, was intended to
minimize cost and provide more immediate
feedback of sounds to the user, and was
connected with a "Music Machine," also built
at the University of Illinois.

230. Dodge, Charles M. The composition of *Changes* and
its computer performance. Diss., Columbia
University, 1970. *UM*71-6164. *Dissertation
Abstracts* 31 (1970-71), 4816A.

231. _____. "Computer generation of human vocal
sound." *Proceedings of the American Society
of University Composers* 6 (1971), 40-45.

Description of the author's preliminary
investigation of computer-generated vocal
sounds, using programs written at Bell
Laboratories by Joseph Olive. The procedure
is synthesis-by-analysis, and one-sentence
examples are presented and described. Hope
is held for a system that will be usable for
composers wishing to make use of texts in
digital synthesis.

Dodge, continued

232. _____. "Synthesizing speech." *Music Journal*
34 (Feb. 1976), 14, 44.

The potential of synthetic speech as a
medium for musical composition is discussed.
Examples are drawn from the author's recent
work *In Celebration* to demonstrate several
possibilities.

233. Douglas, Alan. "Electrical synthesis of music."
Electronics and Power 10 (1964), 83-86.

Includes early report on work then being
done at Bell Laboratories, leading to the
MUSIC IV program and the recording DL9103
"Music from Mathematics."

234. _____. "Electronic music production."
Musical Times 114, 13 (March 1973), 265.

235. Ducasse, Henri. "Compte-rendu du Journées d'Études
d'Informatique Musicale." *Informatique et
Sciences Humaines* 19 (Dec. 1973), 67-70.

Summary of events of a convention sponsored
by the Institut des Sciences Humaines at
the Sorbonne which was concerned with the
use of computers in music.

236. Dunn, John. A hybrid approach in the esthetic
use of computer tools. Paper presented to
the 57th convention of the Audio Engineering
Society, Los Angeles, May 10-13, 1977.

A description is given of a studio utilizing
a microcomputer interfaced with a large E-mu
audio synthesizer and with Sandin and Rutt-
Etra video synthesizers at the Art Institute
of Chicago. Excerpts of work composed with

the system were presented.

237. Dworak, Paul Edward. A input interface for the
real-time control of musical parameters.
Paper presented at the First International
Conference on Computer Music, Massachussetts
Institute of Technology, Oct. 28-31, 1976.

A keyboard-like interface to a system for
real-time digital synthesis at Carnegie-
Mellon University is presented. The keyboard
is position-sensitive, the programmable interface is controlled by high-speed microprocessors, and the system may be interfaced
with a minicomputer to provide external program control.

238. Easton, Robert. "Synthesis of moving sound sources."
Journal of the Audio Engineering Society
19, 5 (May 1971), 443. Abstract.

A system for synthesis of movement in sound
is described. Unique features of the system
include its ability to handle eight or more
different programs simultaneously; to permit
digital control of signal distribution and
rate of apparent motion; and to be workable
in large environments. Construction, principles
of operation, and psychoacoustical phenomena
are discussed.

239. Ehle, Robert C. "Synthesizers, anyone?" *Music
Educators Journal* 57, 5 (Jan. 1971), 78-82.

Synthesizers, computer systems, hybrid systems,
and their price ranges are listed. A short
discussion of Mathews' MUSIC V program for
sound synthesis and the expenses of its
implementation is included.

240. Ehresman, David; and David L. Wessel. Perception
     of timbral analogies. Centre Georges Pompidou
     Rapports IRCAM no. 13, Paris, 1978.

     The "transposition" of timbre melodies was
     studied in the context of a "timbre space"
     representation of synthesized instrument-like
     sounds. Conclusions were drawn from the judge-
     ments made by various listeners in comparing
     timbres and a perceptual model is proposed.

241. Eimert, Herbert; and Hans Ulrich Humpert. *Das
     Lexikon der elektronischen Musik*. Regensburg:
     Gustav Bosse Verlag, 1973.

242. "E.M.A.MU. (Equipe de Mathematique et d'Automa-
     tique Musicales)." *La Revue Musicale* 265-
     266 (1969), 53-59.

     The research center founded in 1967 by
     M. Barbut, F. Genuys, G. Th. Guilbaud, and
     I. Xenakis is described. Its activities, fu-
     ture plans, and equipment (including an IBM
     360 computer) are listed.

243. Emmerson, Simon. "Electronic studios in Britain."
     Music and Musicians 23, 11 (July 1975),
     24-26.

244. Erickson, Raymond F. "The computer and music."
     *Journal of the American Musicological Soci-
     ety* 25 (1972), 102-107.

     Review of *The Computer and Music,* ed. by
     Harry B. Lincoln.

245. _____. DARMS: a reference manual (1976).
     Unpublished manuscript. Queens College,
     Flushing, N.Y.

246. _____. "The DARMS project: a status report." *Computers and the Humanities* 9 (1975), 291–298.

Description of a programming language for representing musical notation, known as DARMS (Digital Alternate Representation of Musical Scores) devised by S. Bauer-Mengelberg.

247. _____. "Music and the computer in the sixties." *AFIPS* [American Federation of Signal Processing] *Conference Proceedings* 36 (1970), 281–285.

Overall survey of work being done in the areas of acoustics, sound synthesis, composition, bibliographies, concordances, and stylistic analyses. An evaluation is given and some problems with several projects are discussed.

248. _____. "The uses of computers in music: a state of the art report." *Proceedings of the First U.S.A.-- Japan Computer Conference.* Tokyo: American Federation of Information Processing Societies, Inc.; Information Processing Society of Japan, 1972. 124–129.

Discussion of a bibliography for computer applications in music, computer-composed and computer-synthesized music, bibliographical applications, and computer-aided analysis. Standards are offered, by which the computer-oriented research ought to be judged. Several ways in which the computer industry can assist humanistic research are suggested.

249. _____; and Anthony B. Wolff. "The DARMS projects: implementation of an artificial language for representation of music." In *Advances in Computers,* ed. by Walter Sedelow

and Sally W. Sedelow. The Hague: Moulton, in press.

Description of the syntax of DARMS.

250. Erickson, Robert. *Sound Structure in Music.* Berkeley: University of California Press, 1975.

251. Espelien, Rune H. Man/machine communications and computer music synthesis. Paper presented at the 49th convention of the Audio Engineering Society, New York, Sept. 9-12, 1974. Preprint No. 997.

A software system for sound synthesis, based on a simplification of MUSIC V, developed at the University of Norway, is described. Peripherals include a graphical input device and a teletype writer.

253. Evans, Stanford. "The aural perception of mathematical structures." *Proceedings of the American Society of University Composers* 6 (1971), 46-48.

The author proposes that with the advent of digital synthesis, mathematical structures made of musical parameters can produce the phonology, syntax, and semantics of a sound experience.

254. Experiments in Art and Technology, Inc. *E.A.T. news.* [New York State Council on the Arts, New York]. 1967-68.

A newsletter of the activities of this organization (E.A.T.),whose members included R. Breer, R. Rauschenberg, R. Whitman, W. Kluver, and others, and which was responsible for some early projects involving art, music, and engineering. Vol. 2, no. 1 related.

254. Federkow, G. See Buxton, Fogels, Federkow, Smith, and Sasaki.

255. _____; William Buxton; and K.C. Smith. "A computer-controlled sound distribution system for the performance of electronic music." *Computer Music Journal* 2, 3 (Dec. 1978), 33-42.

Considerations in the simulation of perceptual cues by which events are located in acoustical space are discussed. A system which incorporates these cues, developed at the University of Toronto, is presented. Other systems which have provisions for directional cues are also described. A complete list of references on sound localization is included.

256. Fencl, Zdeněk. "Počítač jako hudební nastroj." *Hudební věda* [Czech.] 5 (1968), 101-116.

Stochastic composition is discussed. (Summaries in English, German, Russian.)

257. _____. "Komponující algorithmus a obsah informace." *Kybernetika* 2 (1966), 243.

Rules of composition programmed as a restraining condition on random data are discussed.

258. Ferentz, Melvin. See Bauer-Mengelberg and Ferentz.

259. Ferentzy, E.N. "On formal music analysis-synthesis: its application in music education." *Computational Linguistics* 4 (1965), 107.

260. _____; and M. Havass. "Human movement ana-
      lysis by computer-- electronic choreography
      and music composition." *Computational Lin-
      guistics* 3 (1964), 129-188.

      Concerns analysis of dance movements, dance
      and music inter-relations in modern dances,
      with Markov analysis (and composition) of
      choreographies and music as one approach.
      Musical data was introduced through an
      analyzer, which registered amplitude, and
      an 'on-line piano,' which signalled attacks.

261. Ferguson, Lee. "A polyphonic music synthesizer
      utilizing master programmed electronic syn-
      thesis modules for each key." *Journal of the
      Audio Engineering Society* 25, 9 (Sept. 1977),
      592-595.

      A system is described which includes individ-
      ual formant/amplitude shapers and separate
      processing modules, with auto-preset and
      manual programmers, for each key of the
      keyboard.

262. Ferretti, Ercolino. "The computer as a tool for
      the creative musician." In *Computers for the
      Humanities?* New Haven: Yale University Press,
      1965. 109-112.

      Paper delivered at a conference sponsored by
      Yale University on a grant from IBM, Jan. 22-
      23, 1965.

263. _____. "Exploration and organization of
      sound with the computer." *Journal of the
      Acoustical Society of America* 39, 6 (June
      1966), 1245. Abstract.

      Presented to the 71st meeting of the American Acoustical Society.

Computer coding techniques based on the parameters of waveforms are described.

264. _____. Intensity characteristics of a syn-
thesis model for producing brass sounds.
Paper presented at the First International
Conference on Computer Music, Massachussetts
Institute of Technology, Oct. 28-31, 1976.

Characteristics of intensity vs. applied
pressure in performance of brass instruments
are related to digital synthesis of brass
sounds.

265. _____. "Some research notes on music with
the computer." *Proceedings of the First
Meeting of the American Society of University Composers* 1 (1966), 38-41.

Analysis and synthesis of musical sounds
and techniques of coding are discussed.

266. _____. "Sound synthesis by rule." In *Software Synthesis Techniques,* Proceedings of
the Second Annual Music Computation Conference, Nov. 7-9, 1975. Part 1. Urbana: University of Illinois, 1975. 1-21.

Discussion of digital sound synthesis according to mathematical models representing musical instrument tones. Non-periodicity and
"beating" in acoustic instruments is taken
into account. Graphs included.

267. Foerster, H. von. "Sounds and music." In *Music
by Computers,* ed. by H. von Foerster and
J.W. Beauchamp. New York: Wiley and Sons,
1969. 3-10.

Sound as a signature of its source and as an abstract symbol is discussed. The computer is seen to assume a logical role in the history of Western music.

268. _____; and J.W. Beauchamp, eds. *Music by Computers*. New York: Wiley and Sons, 1969.

A collection of essays, divided into three parts: I. Programs and Systems, II. Algorithms in Composition, and III. Aesthetics. See entries for M. David Freedman; A. Roberts; J.W. Beauchamp; L. Hiller; M. Mathews and L. Rosler; H. Brün; J.K. Randall; J.R. Pierce and M. Mathews; G. Strang; and Foerster. Four discs are also included, demonstrating work of the essayists here: *Cosahedron* by L. Hiller; *Infraudibles* by H. Brün; *The British Grenadiers-- Johnny Comes Marching Home* and *International Lullabye* by M. Mathews; *Eight-Tone Cannon* by John Pierce; examples of synthesized instrumental tones compared with acoustic original tones by J.W. Beauchamp; work in progress by G. Strang; *Sonatina for CDC-3600, Title Music to LINK,* and *Rocket* by A. Roberts; and *Variation 6-10 (1966)* by J.K. Randall.

269. Fogels, E.A. See Buxton, Fogels, Federkow, Smith, and Sasaki.

270. Fornango, James. See Beauchamp and Fornango.

271. Fornůsek, Jaroslav. "Aplikace zkušenosti z projektování úloh na samočinném počítači pro oblast lidové písně." *Lidova´písen a samočinný počítač I,* ed. by Dušan Holý and Oldřich Sirovátka. Brno: Klub uživatelů MSP, 1972. 11-12.

Report on research in progress.

272. Forte, Allen. "Music and computing: the present situation." *Computers and the Humanities* 2 (1967-68), 32-35.

An expanded version also appears in *AFIPS* [American Federation for Information Processing] *Conference Proceedings* 31 (1967), 327-329.

An overview of current uses of computers in music, as of 1967, for projects in composition, analysis, research, and bibliographical applications.

273. _____. *SNOBOL 3 Primer: An Introduction to the Computer Programming Language.* Cambridge: MIT Press, 1967.

This book was intended as a textbook for the musician who wants to learn the computer language SNOBOL, a language particularly well-suited for musical purposes and humanistic research in general.

Reviewed in *Computers and the Humanities* 2, 5 (2968), 256-262. Several ambiguous points in the *SNOBOL 3 Primer* are explained (concerning statements on pp. 22, 65, 45, and 61).

274. Franco, Sergio. Hardware design of a real-time musical system. Diss., University of Illinois, 1974. 96 pp.

Also, as University of Illinois Department of Computer Science Technical Report No. R-74-677.

Description of hardware design of a hybrid digital-analog system for live performance of electronic music. Sound generation and processing employ analog circuitry. Digital controls may be pre-set and overridden at any time by the performer. The work was done in collaboration with composer Salvatore Martirano. (The instrument described is otherwise known as the SalMar Construction.)

275. Franke, Herbert W. *Computergraphik-computerkunst.* München: Bruckmann, 1971. 136 pp.

Outline of the history of computer art. The input and output apparatus, theories behind computer art, and the adaptation of calculus to the presentation of aesthetic orders are discussed. The use of computers in graphics, film, music and poetry are presented.

276. Freedman, M. David. "A digital computer for the electronic music studio." *Journal of the Audio Engineering Society* 15 (1967), 43-50.

Several schemes for music synthesis are presented. A discussion of hardware, software, and peripheral devices required for real-time generation of sound follows. Appendices on memory requirements for central processing units and some timing considerations are included.

277. _____. "Analysis of musical instrument tones." *Journal of the Acoustical Society of America* 41 (1967), 793-806.

A technique for the analysis of musical instrument tones is presented. The end result is a mathematical representation of the tone being investigated. Inharmonic frequencies were detected and utilized in this experimentation with trumpet, saxophone, violin, bassoon, and clarinet tones, employing the

Illiac II computer at the University of Illinois.

278. _____. "On-line generation of sound." In *Music by Computers*, ed. By H. von Foerster and J.W. Beauchamp. New York: Wiley & Sons, 1969. 13-18.

The essential specifications for any computer system for synthesis of tones and analysis of musical instrument tones are presented. Suggestions for interfaces allowing interactive control of the system are made.

279. _____. "Slewing distortion in digital-to-analog conversion." *Journal of the Audio Engineering Society* 25, 4 (1977), 178-183.

Report on research on the problem of producing high quality sound signals from digital input, in computer music applications.

280. _____. "Technique for the analysis of musical instrument tones." *Journal of the Acoustical Society of America* 38, 11 (1965), 912. Abstract.

Also, as University of Illinois Biological Computer Laboratory Technical Report No. 6 (10718) Urbana, Ill., 1965. 146 pp.

Also, as A Technique for the Analysis of Musical Instrument Tones. Diss., University of Illinois, 1965. 146 pp. *Dissertation Abstracts* 26, 12 (June 1966), 7216.

A high-speed digital computer is used to analyze attack transients of musical tones and the conclusions are verified by resynthesis of the tones, employing the facilities at the University of Illinois.

281. Friedman, Richard. See Buchla and Friedman.

282. Friend, David. "A time-shared hybrid synthesizer."
Journal of the Audio Engineering Society 19,
11 (Dec. 1971), 928-935.

The author, from ARP Instruments, outlines a
plan for a synthesizer controlled by a small
computer, with simplified composer notations,
time-sharing facilities, and remote score-
reading and playback facilities at other
institutions. This work is based on the operation of the Mark II synthesizer (RCA) and
CYTOS (Conversational Yale Time-Sharing Operations System).

283. _____. The ARP PRO Soloist Synthesizer.
Paper presented at the 46th convention of
the Audio Engineering Society, New York,
Sept. 10-13, 1973. Preprint.

Discussion of LSI circuitry used to store
information pertaining to the production of
thirty preset instrumental sounds in this
model of ARP synthesizer.

284. Gabura, James; and Gustav Ciamaga. "Computer
control of sound apparatus for electronic
music." *Journal of the Audio Engineering
Society* 16, 1 (Jan. 1968), 49-51.

A method of sound generation combining digital and analog techniques for accurate and
economic realization of electronic compositions is described.

285. _____. "Digital computer control of sound generating apparatus for the production of electronic music." *Electronic Music Review* 1 (Jan. 1967), 54-57.

A method is described by which a computer provides control voltages for analog equipment, making a five-part texture possible without multiple recording and dubbing techniques.

286. Gardner, John; Brian Harvey; James R. Lawson; and Jean-Claude Risset. Computer facilities for music at IRCAM, as of October 1977. Centre Georges Pompidou Rapports IRCAM No. 3, Paris, 1978.

Also presented at the 1977 International Computer Music Conference, University of California, San Diego, Cal.

The projected goals and current status of the IRCAM (Institut de Recherche et Coordination Acoustique/Musique) computer system, with reference to both hardware and software, is described. Brief mention is made of various user and system level programs.

287. Gena, Peter. Musicol Manual, Version I. National Science Foundation Project No. GK-14191, Technical Report No. 7, Buffalo, New York, May 1973.

Users' manual for program run on a CDC 6400 computer at the State University of New York in Buffalo. Conventional musical notation in a free-card format is allowed for data input.

288. Ghent, Emmanuel. Computer-generated electronic lighting synthesis. Paper presented at the 42nd convention of the Audio Engineering Society, Los Angeles, May 2-5, 1972.

The GROOVE program developed by Max Mathews at Bell Laboratories has been applied here to lighting control for a new dimension in performance and synchronization of light with electronic sound composition.

289. _____. Real-time interactive compositional procedures. Paper read at the First International Conference on Computer Music, Massachussetts Institute of Technology, Oct. 28-31, 1976.

Various compositional procedures using Mathews's GROOVE system to create musical lines with pitches and rhythms selected through operations of probability are described.

290. _____. "Programmed signals to performers: a new compositional resource." *Perspectives of New Music* 6, 1 (Fall-Winter 1967), 96-106.

The rhythmic structure of a composition is translated to real-time values on punched cards and converted to multiplexed 8-channel audio signals. The purpose is to cue performers in elaborate rhythmic structures coordinated with electronically-generated taped material. Future projects are described.

291. Gill, S. "A technique for the composition of music in a computer." *Computer Journal* 6, 2 (July 1963), 29-31.

A system for a Pegasus computer, using random number compositional processes and transcription of the printout into musical notation, is described.

292. Gish, Walter C. Analysis and synthesis of musical instrument tones. Paper presented at the
61st meeting of the Audio Engineering Society, New York, Nov. 3-6, 1978.

An analysis technique, by which tones whose
partial structure is inharmonic and time-
variant may be studied and reproduced, is
discussed here.

293. Gold, Rich. See Bischoff, Gold, Horton.

294. Gordon, John W.; and John M. Grey. "Perception
of spectral modifications on orchestral
instrument tones." *Computer Music Journal*
2, 1 (July 1978), 24-31.

Two experiments on the perception of timbre,
involving the use of a multidimensional scaling technique, in conjunction with digital
analysis and re-synthesis of instrumental
tones, are discussed. Graphs, charts, and
bibliography included.

295._____. See Grey, J.M., and Gordon.

296. Gould, Murray. "Computer synthesis of music in
the New York area: a report." *Contemporary
Music Newsletter* 2, 1 (Jan. 1968), 2-5.

Survey of current work being done at Columbia
University, Queens College, and elsewhere
in the metropolitan area.

297. Green, D.H. See Powner, Green and Taylor.

298. Gressel, Joel. "Some rhythmic applications of geometric series." In *Composition with Computers*, Proceedings of the Second Annual Music Computation Conference, Nov. 7-9, 1975, part 2. Urbana: University of Illinois, 1975. 11-30.

Attack patterns derived from the geometric series are used as data for a sound synthesis program, creating rhythmic augmentation-diminution, exponential relationships, rhythmic retrograde, and other relationships.

299. _____. Variable amplitude modulation by BUZZ. Paper read at the First International Conference on Computer Music, Massachussetts Institute of Technology, Oct. 28-31, 1976.

A compositional technique is described: the unit generator of the programs MUSIC 4BF and MUSIC 360 is ring-modulated to produce interesting spectral changes.

300. Grey, John M. An Exploration of Musical Timbre. Diss., Stanford University, 1975.

Also, as Stanford University Department of Music Technical Report STAN-M-2.

Computer analysis and synthesis of orchestral instrument tones was used as an approach to the study of timbre perception. It was found that naturalistic tones could be simulated using a much simplified set of physical properties, aiding in psychophysical interpretations of data on human perception of sound.

301. _____. "Multidimensional perceptual scaling of musical timbre." *Journal of the Acoustical Society of America* 61, 5 (May 1977), 1270-1277.

Experiments in computer analysis and synthesis of musical instrument tones were made. Data from perceptual judgements made by subjects are treated with multidimensional scaling techniques and analyzed. Charts, graphs, and bibliography included.

302. _____; and J. Gordon. "Perception of spectral modifications of orchestral instrument timbres." *Journal of the Acoustical Society of America* 63, 5 (May 1978), 1493-1500.

A Stanford University experiment employing computer analysis-synthesis of musical instrument tones was performed to evaluate the effects of controlled spectral modifications on a set of timbres. The data gathered from subjects' judgements are analyzed here.

303. _____; and J.A. Moorer. "Perceptual evaluations of synthesized musical instrument tones." *Journal of the Acoustical Society of America* 62, 2 (Aug. 1977), 454-462.

Analysis-based synthesis technique for computer generation of musical instrument tones was perceptually evaluated. Certain small details in the attack segments of tones were pinpointed as important factors. An attempt to simplify the required input data was made and it was found that a line-segment approximation of the functions for each partial of a tone was successful.

304. _____. See Chowning, Grey, Moorer, and Rush.

305. _____. See Gordon and Grey.

306. _____. See Moorer and Grey.

307. _____. See Wessel and Grey.

308. Griese, J.; and E. Werner. Vocoder techniques for synthetic and voice-controlled sound generation. Paper presented at the 56th convention of the Audio Engineering Society, Paris, March 1-4, 1977.

   A special version of the vocoder offering additional effects for use by musicians was described. Recorded examples were presented.

309. Grogono, Peter. "MUSYS-- software for an electronic music studio." *Software Practice and Experience* 3, 4 (Oct.-Dec. 1973), 369-383.

   MUSYS is a system of programs used to create music at the computer studio of Electronic Music Studios, London. This paper describes the programming language and the implementation of the compiler and other programs in the system. The system employs a PDP/8 computer and hardware designed by David Cockerell, with the software designed by Peter Zinovieff and the author. Programmed control voltages are to be used with an oscillator bank, noise generator, and "percussion simulator." Further developments of the system are mentioned and a list of compositions produced with the system is given. This list includes work by H. Birtwistle, J. Connolly, D. Rowland, and H.W. Henze.

310. Gross, Robert. "The CME Synthesizer." In *Hard-ware for Computer-Controlled Sound Synthesis,* Proceedings of the Second Annual Music Computation Conference, Nov. 7-9, 1975, part 4. Urbana: University of Illinois, 1975. 37-42.

Description of a proposed digital synthesizer to be designed and built at the University of California Center for Music Experiment at San Diego by Bruce Leibig, Bruce Rittenbach, Robert Fleming, and the author. A PDP-11/20 computer will be utilized, along with microprocessors, and additional hardware-- a multiprocessing approach.

311. Grossi, Pietro. "Computer and music." *International Review of Aesthetics and Social Musicology* 4, 2 (1973), 279-86.

312. _____. Musical Studies I-- instruction manual of DCMP. Pisa: University of Pisa, 1970. 20 pp. English trans. by Anna M. Burney.

Program will store diatonic sequence of tones for a single voice, modify them, and execute them in real time. The program is run on an IBM 360/30, 360/44, or 7090 computer.

313. _____. Outline of the research at the CNUCE-CNR of Pisa, Italy. Paper read at the First International Conference on Computer Music, Massachussetts Institute of Technology, Oct. 28-31, 1976.

Operative procedures of the three main programs in use for sound synthesis at the CNUCE music department are presented. Hardware includes an IBM 370/168 system, IBM system/7, and a specially built audio-terminal.

314. Grossman, Gary. "A computer sound generation program allowing the use of user-defined production algorithms." *Journal of the Audio Engineering Society* 15, 1 (1967), 96. Abstract.

Description of a program for the Illiac II computer at the University of Illinois allowing signal computation algorithms in FORTRAN-like language, loading and scanning of waveform samples, and definition of compositional functions. Problems of foldover and computer size memory are discussed.

315. _____; and James Cuomo. "Provisional sound generator." In Four Sound Processing Programs for the Illiac II computer and D/A converter, ed. James W. Beauchamp. University of Illinois Experimental Music Studio Technical Report No. 14, Urbana, Sept. 1968. 50-68.

316. _____. See Beauchamp, Grossman, Otis, and Cuomo.

317. Groupe Art et Informatique. *Artinfo/Musinfo.* [Université Paris VIII, France]. N.d.

Technical bulletins of the French computer arts association Groupe Art et Informatique de Vincennes.

318. Gruhn, Wilfried. "Elektronische Musik im Unterricht." *Musik und Bildung* 2, 1 (June 1970), 6-10.

319. Guttman, N. "Notes on computer music examples."
Gravesaner Blätter 23-24 (1962), 126-131.
Parallel German and English texts.

Description of early work done by Max Mathews
and the author at Bell Laboratories in digital sound synthesis.

320. _____. See Mathews and Guttman.

321. _____. See Mathews, Guttman, and Pierce.

322. Haflich, Steven. Computer on-line music editing
in a compositional environment: some special
considerations. Paper presented at the
First International Conference on Computer
Music, Massachussetts Institute of Technology, Oct. 28-31, 1976.

Presentation of a system at MIT for typing
in standard musical notation on a cathode
ray tube screen so that the composer may
rearrange, change, and otherwise edit his
score and then have it performed through
the digital synthesis system.

323. Hafner, Everett. Computers, synthesizers, and
the physics of music. Proceedings of the
Fourth Annual Conference on Computing,
Claremont, Cal., June 1973. 309-318.

Use of a system for study of acoustics at
Hampshire College, Massachussetts, is described here. The Synthi AKS synthesizer is
used in conjunction with programmed control.
Exercises produced at the college are given
as examples.

324. Hamm, Russell O. Fast pitch detection. Paper presented at the 58th convention of the Audio Engineering Society, New York, Nov. 4-7, 1977. Preprint No. 1265.

The development of digital and analog systems for extracting pitch information from musical waveforms is discussed. A new pitch algorithm has been developed which can be executed in real-time with digital circuitry.

325. Hansen, Finn Egeland. "Elektrofoni og konkret musik." *Actuel Musik*. Copenhagen: Danmarks Radio, 1968.

326. _____. "1975 in review and plans for 1976." *Electronic Music and Musical Acoustics* [Aarhus: Institute of Musicology], 1 (1975), 108-109.

Brief listing of projects in digital synthesis at the University of Aarhus.

327. _____. "1976 in review, plans for 1977." *Electronic Music and Musical Acoustics* [Aarhus], 2 (1976), 110-111.

Brief listing of projects.

328. _____. "1977 in review, plans for 1978." *Electronic Music and Musical Acoustics* [Aarhus], 3 (1977), 94-95.

List of activities, including development of digital synthesizer.

329. _____. "Sonic demonstration of the EGG Synthesizer." *Electronic Music and Musical Acoustics* [Aarhus], 3 (1977), 5-48.

A brief summary of the command language is
given here for this digital synthesizer
developed at the University of Aarhus. Sample
sound patterns produced by the synthesizer
are described in full and recorded on a
cassette which accompanies this issue.

330. _____. "TI 960A minicomputeren på Musik-
videnskabeligt Institut." In 3 foredrag over
emnet: Autonome computere herunder minicom-
putere og deres anvendelse i forbindelse med
regionale edbcentre. University of Aarhus
Technical Report RECAU-74-39, Aarhus, 1974.

331. Harasek, Richard. The Scalatron: a digitally
programmable keyboard instrument. Paper
presented at the Midwest Acoustics Conference, Evanston, Ill., April 5, 1975.

The Scalatron is described here as an instrument that can be tuned to any scale of
24 steps per octave or less. Accuracy is
assured by the use of digital circuitry.

332. Harvey, Brian. See Gardner, Harvey, Lawson, and
Risset.

333. Hastings, Chuck. "A recipe for homebrew ECL."
Computer Music Journal 2, 1 (July 1978),
48-59.

Emitter-coupled logic (ECL) may be used to
develop a very fast, small computing system
that might be useful for music synthesis and
other computer hobbyist's applications, according to the author. The "recipe" for such
a system is given here. A list of vendors of
the required materials is attached.

334. Hatano, Giyoo. "Ongaku-e-no jōhōren teki sekkin."
     Ongaku gaku 14 (1968), 54-64.

     Previous informational studies upon which
     computer simulation of musical composition
     is based are discussed. The model of music
     as a Markov chain is refuted in favor of
     another model based on Chomsky's idea of
     generative grammar.

335. Havass, M. "A simulation of musical composition."
     In *Computational Linguistics*, vol. III.
     Budapest: Computing Center of the Hungarian
     Academy of Sciences, 1964. 107-127.

     A detailed mathematical description is given
     of a computer program to produce marching
     songs.

336. _____. See Ferentzy and Havass.

337. Haynes, Stanley. Software sound synthesis in the
     United Kingdom. Paper read at the First In-
     ternational Conference on Computer Music,
     Massachussetts Institute of Technology,
     Oct. 28-31, 1976.

     Report on digital sound synthesis in the U.K.
     Principally under discussion is work begun
     at Southampton University in 1972 for imple-
     menting MUSIC 4B and MUSIC V, using an
     ICL 1709 computer and also a CDC 7600 system.
     A new version of MUSIC V for an ICL 2970 sys-
     tem is under development at this time.

338. Heckmann, Harald, ed. *Elektronische Datenver-
     arbeitung in der Musikwissenschaft*.
     Regensburg: Gustav Bosse, 1967. 237 pp.

     Includes article by Thomas E. Binckley. See
     Binckley. Other articles oriented toward

musicology.

339. Heike, Georg. "Informationstheorie und musikalische Komposition." *Melos* 28 (1961), 269-272.

In relating information theory to music, the author cites the work of Meyer-Eppler, Ligeti, Eimert, Adorno, Cage, Stockhausen, and Koenig.

340. Helm, Everett. "UNESCO report on the Stockholm meeting." *Music and Technology*. Paris: La Revue Musicale, 1971. 193-206.

Also as "Rapport de l'UNESCO sur la reunion de Stockholm." *La Revue Musicale,* 268-269 (1971), 195-208.

A summary of papers presented at a meeting in Stockholm on the topic of music and technology. Ensuing discussions by other composers and conclusions regarding electronic and computer music are printed.

341. Helmers, Carl. "Add a klugeharp to your computer." *Byte* 1, 2 (Oct. 1975), 14.

Presented as an interesting diversion, a tone generator is improvised as a peripheral for a Motorola 6800 microprocessor, using the device designed for testing the system. Program loops produce the tones.

342. Hemingway, Bruce; and David K. Barton. Microprocessors: a multiprocessing approach to real-time digital sound synthesis. Paper presented at the First International Conference on Computer Music, Massachussetts Institute of Technology, Oct. 28-31, 1976.

A system which employs eight microprocessors, allowing the flexibility of a large scale computer system, is being developed for real-time digital synthesis at Indiana University at South Bend, Indiana. Timing and other data functions are assigned so as to overcome speed limitations of the microprocessors, providing the composer with "choirs" of synthetic instruments.

343. Henke, W.L. Musical Interactive Tone Synthesis System. Cambridge: Massachussetts Institute of Technology, 1970. Mimeo.

Description of interactive digital synthesis system under development at M.I.T.

344. _____. "Two-dimensional notations for the specification of sound and music synthesis." *Journal of the Acoustical Society of America* 50, 1/part 1 (July 1971), 128. Abstract.

An interactive system utilizing a PDP-9 computer and a synthesizer, called MITSYN, is under development at Massachussetts Institute of Technology. The system, the parameter files and the program's graphical notations are described.

345. Hibino, Masahiro; and Kenji Shima. A 16-channel real-time music synthesizer. Paper presented at the 61st convention of the Audio Engineering Society, New York, Nov. 3-6, 1978.

A digital synthesizer has been developed at Mitsubishi Electric Corp., Tokyo, which employs waveform generators with resistive plates and a microcomputer. Score input equipment includes an optical mark card reader and a digital cassette recorder.

346. Higgins, D. "Does Avant-Garde Mean Anything?"
Arts in Society 7, 1 (1970), 28-31.

In his discussion of the diversity of modern
composition, the author considers computer
composition.

347. Hijman, Julius. "Elektronisch componeren?" *Mens
en Melodie* 16 (1961), 141-145.

Introduction to the use of computers in
composition.

348. Hillen, Peter. " . . . how computers talk to
synthesizers." *Synapse* 1, 3 (Sept.-Oct.
1976), 3.

Short introductory explanation of A/D and
D/A conversion in computer-synthesizer
interfaces.

349. _____. "How computers store numbers."
Synapse 1, 4 (Nov.-Dec. 1976), 4.

Short lesson on the binary system.

350. _____. "The link between computers and
synthesizers." *Synapse* 1, 5 (Jan.-Feb. 1977),
4.

Lesson on D/A conversion: explanation of
terms full-scale and resolution. Specification of a D/A converter suitable for synthesizers is then derived.

351. _____. "The link between computers and synthesizers, part 2." *Synapse* 1, 6 (March/A-
pril 1977), 32.

Formulae for the operation of a D/A converter
are explained.

352. _____. "Using an A/D converter." *Synapse* 2, 3 (Nov.-Dec. 1977), 49.

Explanation of sampling rate and use of sample-and-hold function in an A/D converter.

353. _____. "S/H and A/D conversion." *Synapse* 2, 4 (Jan.-Feb. 1978), 30.

Explanation of sample-and-hold circuitry (its role in A/D conversion having been discussed previously).

354. _____. "Digital delay lines." *Synapse* 2, 5 (March-April 1978), 41.

Explanation of digital delay lines.

355. _____. A microprocessor-based sequencer for voltage-controlled electronic music synthesizers. Paper presented at the 57th convention of the Audio Engineering Society, Los Angeles, May 10-13, 1977. Preprint no. 1229.

The system described includes a microprocessor, computer terminal input, and digital-to-analog converter output. The microprocessor is interfaced with a voltage-controlled oscillator.

356. Hiller, Lejaren. *Analysis and Synthesis of Musical Sounds by Analog and Digital Techniques; an interim progress report to the National Science Foundation.* Urbana: University of Illinois Press, 1967.

This report contains information on the revised MUSICOMP manual, principles of sound analysis and resynthesis, musical instrument analysis and resynthesis, analog studio equipment and related research, teaching programs, and publication.

357. _____. Composition with hierarchical structures. Paper presented at the Second Annual Music Computation Conference, Urbana, Ill., Nov. 7-9, 1975.

Description of a program called PHRASE, which deals with groups of notes rather than single note parameters, and an orchestra score produced with this program.

358. _____. "Computer music." *Scientific American* 201, 6 (Dec. 1959), 109-120.

Early experiments leading up to the *Illiac Suite* for string quartet are described in general terms. The 'Monte Carlo' method and Markoff probability chains, used in this work, are also treated in a non-technical discussion.

359. _____. "Computer music." In *Cybernetic Serendipity*, ed. Jasia Reichardt. New York: Frederick A. Praeger, 1969. 21-23.

Similar to preceding article.

360. _____. Computer programs used to produce the composition *HPSCHD*. National Science Foundation Project No. GK-14191 Technical Report No. 4, Buffalo, New York, Aug. 1972. 205-213.

361. _____. "Electronic and computer music." *St. Louis Post-Dispatch*, May 7, 1969, 5C.

362. _____. "Electronic synthesis of microtonal music." *Proceedings of the American Society of University Composers* 2 (1967), 99-106.

The use of scales other than the chromatic
scale in the electronic media is discussed,
with examples from the author's *Seven Electronic Studies (1963)*. The author concludes
that the computer provides a more elegant
means of producing these scales.

363. _____. "These electrons go round and round
and come out music." *IRE Student Quarterly*
8, 1 (Sept. 1961), 36-45.

364. _____. Information theory and musical
analysis. University of Illinois Experimental
Music Studio Technical Report No. 5, Urbana,
Illinois, July 1962.

365. _____. *Informationstheorie und Computermusik*. Mainz: B. Schott's Söhne, 1964.
(Darmstadter Beiträge zur Neuen Musik, 8).
62 pp.

A fairly complete description is given of
the *Computer Cantata*, a composition produced
by Hiller and Leonard Isaacson with the use
of the Illiac II and programming which
assumes a relationship between information
theories and music.

366. _____. Music composed with computers-- an
historical survey. University of Illinois
Experimental Music Studio Technical Report
No. 18, Urbana, Illinois, Feb. 1968.

Also, as "Music composed with computers-- a
historical survey." In *The Computer and
Music*, ed. Harry B. Lincoln. Ithaca: Cornell
University Press, 1970. 42-96.

A report on international research to date,
including the use of composition programs
and sound generation by digital means.

367. _____. "Musical applications of electronic digital computers." *Gravesaner Blätter* 27-28 (Nov. 1965), 62-72.

A brief non-technical review of the use of the digital computer in sound-generation, score printing, analysis, and composition. An outline for the yet uncompleted *Second Illiac Suite* is presented.

368. _____. "Muzyczne zastowanie elektronowych muszyn cyfrowych." *Ruch Muzyczny* 6, 7 (April 15, 1962), 11-13.

369. _____. On the use of a high speed electronic digital computer for musical composition. MM thesis, University of Illinois, 1958. 174 pp.

370. _____. "Programming a computer for musical composition." In *Papers from the West Virginia Conference on Computer Applications in Music,* ed. Gerald Lefkoff. Morgantown: West Virginia University Library, 1967. 65-88.

A technical description of the program MUSICOMP, developed at the University of Illinois for use by composers, is described here. Graphical illustrations of the structure of the *Computer Cantata,* a composition produced with this program, are included.

371. _____. "Programming the I-Ching oracle." *Computer Studies in the Humanities and Verbal Behavior* 3, 3 (Oct. 1970), 130-143.

The subroutine ICHING, used in the Hiller-Cage collaboration *HPSCHD,* was written in SCATRE, an assembly language for the IBM 7094 computer, and is described here in detail. Tables of the 64 hexagrams, statistics on their probabilities

and permutations, flow-charts for the
various subroutines, and graphs of the
frequency distribution are included.

372. _____. Report on contemporary experimental
music, 1961. University of Illinois Experimental Music Studio Technical Report No. 4,
Urbana, Ill., June 1962. 92 pp.

The development of electronic music instruments is briefly summarized and recent
European music is discussed. Applications
of the computer as a musical instrument
at the University of Illinois and in Europe
are summarized also. References are included.

373. _____. *Seven Electronic Studies for Two-
Channel Tape Recorder (1963).* University
of Illinois Experimental Music Studio
Technical Report No. 6, Urbana, Ill.,
May 1963. 73 pp.

374. _____. "Some comments on computer sound
synthesis." *Proceedings of the First
Meeting of the American Society of University Composers.* Princeton: Princeton
University, 1966. 47-48.

Analysis of musical sounds is suggested
as a starting point for composition with
computers. Digital storage of electronic
music and hybrid digital-analog systems
are seen as the most effective and practical
uses of the computer in composition for the
future.

375. _____. "Some compositional techniques
involving the use of computers." In *Music
by Computers,* ed. H. von Foerster and
J.W. Beauchamp. New York: Wiley and Sons,
1969. 71-83.

Review of activities of 1963-68 and a
detailed discussion of the composition
Algorithmus I and II. This piece was
composed for instruments by programming
selected compositional processes, using a
language for compositional programming
(MUSICOMP) developed by the author and
Robert Baker in 1963. A table of available
MUSICOMP subroutines is given and a
recorded example is included.

376. _____. "Some structural principles of
computer music." *Journal of the American
Musicological Society* 9, 3 (Fall 1956),
247. Abstract.

Abstract of a paper presented in May 1957
on the general principles used in analysis
and composition with the aid of the computer.
The *Illiac Suite* is mentioned.

377. _____. "Z prac Studia Muzyki Eksperymentalnej
University of Illinois." *Horyzonty Musyki*
38 (March 26, 1964), 1-5.

378. _____; and Robert A. Baker. *Computer Cantata:*
a study in composition using the University
of Illinois IBM 7090 and CSX-1 electronic
digital computers. University of Illinois
Experimental Music Studio Technical Report
No. 8, Urbana, Ill., Oct. 1963. 43 pp.

379. _____; _____. "*Computer Cantata:* a study
in compositional method." *Perspectives of
New Music* 3, 1 (Fall-Winter 1964), 62-90.

The composition *Computer Cantata*, produced
by the authors with the Illiac II at the
University of Illinois, is analyzed. The
composition is evaluated as a scientific
experiment and the text is explained and

reproduced here in full. A bibliography is included as well.

380. _____; _____. "Computer music." In *Computer Applications in the Behavioral Sciences*, ed. Harold Borko. Englewood Cliffs: Prentice-Hall, 1962. 424-450.

The *Illiac Suite* is described in detail, including flow-charts for the programming and a hypothesis of compositional procedure based on Schenkerian analysis is proposed.

381. _____; James W. Beauchamp. "Research in music with electronics." *Science* 150 (1965), 161-169.

The historical background of the rational study of music is given, leading up to the use of the computer in music. The studio at the University of Illinois and digital equipment in use there is described, with an overview of the work being carried on, as of 1965.

382. _____; _____. Review of completed and proposed research on analysis and synthesis of musical sounds by analog and digital techniques. University of Illinois Experimental Music Studio Technical Report No. 19, Urbana, Ill., July 1967. 90 pp.

383. _____; J.L. Divilbiss; David Barron; Herbert Brün; Erh Lin. Operators' manual for the 'CSX-1 Music Machine.' University of Illinois Experimental Music Studio Technical Report No. 12, Urbana, Ill., March 1966. 35 pp. Mimeo.

384. _____; Leonard M. Isaacson. *Experimental Music: Composition with an Electronic Computer.* New York, N.Y.: McGraw-Hill, 1959.

The creation of *The Illiac Suite* for string quartet by the authors, employing the Illiac II computer at the University of Illinois in the choice of pitches and rhythms, is described in detail. The nature of experimental music is discussed and the entire project is presented as an experiment. The musical and technical problems and their solutions in this work are set forth, along with the mathematical bases, purposes, and principles embodied in each movement of the composition. The complete score is included in the appendix.

385. _____; _____. "Experimental music." In *The Modelling of the Mind-- Computers and Intelligence.* Notre Dame, In.: University of Notre Dame Press, 1963. 43-71.

Reprint of section from *Experimental Music* by Hiller and Isaacson. New York, N.Y.: McGraw-Hill, 1959.

386. _____; _____. "Musical composition with a high-speed digital computer." *Journal of the Audio Engineering Society* 6, 3 (July 1958), 154-160.

A semi-technical discussion of *The Illiac Suite* is presented. The first page of Experiment No. 3 from the composition, tables and flow-charts for the main routine of Experiments 2 and 3, and a follow-up discussion with members of the Audio Engineering Society are included.

387. _____; and Antonio Leal. Revised MUSICOMP
        manual. University of Illinois Experimental
        Music Studio Technical Report No. 13,
        Urbana, Ill., June 1966. 89 pp. Mimeo.

388. _____; and Pierre Ruiz. "Synthesizing musical
        sounds by solving the wave equation for
        vibrating objects: part 1." *Journal of
        the Audio Engineering Society* 1, 1 (June
        1971), 462-470.

        Presentation of a technique for computer-
        generated sounds, using values obtained
        from differential equations describing
        scintillations of a vibrating object. The
        technique is applied to the simulation of
        vibrating strings. Part 1 deals with the
        computational processes and typical results.
        A bibliography is included.

389. _____; _____. "Synthesizing musical
        sounds by solving the wave equation for
        vibrating objects: part 2." *Journal of the
        Audio Engineering Society* 19, 7 (July/Aug.
        1971), 542-551.

        Also appears in Two Musical Applications
        of Computer Programming, ed. R.F. Brainerd.
        National Science Foundation Project No.
        GK-14191 Technical Report No. 3, Buffalo,
        N.Y., Sept. 1972. 63-71.

        Part 2 includes the solutions to the
        equations set forth in Part 1, digital-to-
        analog conversion of the resulting values,
        and use of a microfilm plotter to record
        several cycles of the solution. Simulation
        of stringed instrument sounds and new sounds
        generated in this way are described and
        recorded on a sound sheet included with
        this issue.

390. Hoffman, Walter, ed. *Digital Information Processors*. New York: Interscience, 1962. 740 pp.

Includes article by Heinz Zemanek, "Automaten und Denkprozesse." See Zemanek.

391. Holý, Dušan; Antonín Bartošík; and Stanislav Zabadal. "Cil-ukoly-postupy-perspektivy." *Lidová písen a samocinný pocítac I*, ed. Dušan Holý and Oldrich Sirovátka. Brno: Klub uživatelu MSP, 1972. 19-43.

392. _____; and Oldrich Sirovátka, eds. *Lidová písen a samocinný pocítac I*. Brno: Klub uzvatelu MSP, 1972. 258 pp.

393. Horton, Jim. See Bischoff, Gold, and Horton.

394. Horvath, Helmuth. "Musik von Computern." *Österreichische Musikzeitschrift* 27 (1972), 573-575.

Review of *Music by Computers*, ed. H. von Foerster and J. W. Beauchamp. New York: Wiley and Sons, 1969.

395. Howe, Hubert S. "The chaotic state of computer music." *Computers and the Humanities* 4, 4 (1969-1970), 277-283.

Also appears in *Perspectives of New Music*, 8, 2 (Spring-Summer 1970), 151-157.

Review of *Music by Computers*, ed. H. von Foerster and J. W. Beauchamp. New York: Wiley and Sons, 1969.

396. _____. "Composing by computer." *Computers and the Humanities* 9, 6 (1975), 281-290.

Earlier version presented at the Second International Conference on Computers and the Humanities at the University of Southern California, April 1975.

Comments on a composer's approach to programming technical devices of his own music and past work. The author describes his own program, based on multidimensional arrays, in some detail. An example of the musical output of the program and some conclusions are offered.

397. _____. "Compositional limitations of electronic music synthesizers." *Perspectives of New Music* 10, 2 (Spring-Summer 1972), 120-129.

Also, appears in *Journal of the Audio Engineering Society* 19, 6 (1971), 484.

Critique of current trends in synthesizer design. The discoveries made recently through digital synthesis of instrument tones are discussed. These lessons are seen to clarify the timbral short-comings of analog synthesizers.

398. _____. "Compositional technique in computer sound synthesis." *Proceedings of the American Society of University Composers* 7-8 (1972/1973), 23-50.

399. _____. "Computer music and technology." In *Composition with Computers,* Proceedings of the Second Annual Music Computation Conference, Nov. 7-9, 1975, part 2. Urbana: University of Illinois, 1975. 31-36.

Reflections on the current state and real priorities of computer music and discussion of some common misconceptions.

400. _____. "Electronic music and microcomputers." *Interface* 7, 1 (May 1978), 57-68.

Overview of recent developments in the field of microcomputers and of musical applications of them. Basic factual information on micro-processing is given, along with a short bibliography of the newer journals devoted to either electronic music or microcomputers.

401. _____. *Electronic Music Synthesis: Concepts, Facilities, Techniques.* New York: Norton, 1975.

This textbook on electronic music introduces digital sound synthesis and includes the user's manual for the author's own program, MUSIC7.

402. _____. "A general view of compositional procedure in computer sound synthesis." *Proceedings of the American Society of University Composers* 3 (1968), 98-108.

Explanation of sound synthesis by means of computers is given to an audience of composers. Reference is made particularly to the MUSIC 4B program. The potential advantages of digital sound synthesis to composers is discussed, along with the limitations and the need to understand the physical basis of timbre.

403. _____. "Letter to the editor." *Computers and the Humanities* 7 (1972-73), 97-98.

404. _____. Multi-dimensional arrays. Diss., Princeton University, 1972. 162 pp. UM72-29790. *Dissertation Abstracts* 33 (1972-73), 2412-A.

Includes a print-out score for the tape
composition *Interchanges*, generated by
the composer's MUSIC7 program, which uses
multi-dimensional arrays as a compositional
technique. The Sigma 7 computer system at
Queens College was used for sound synthesis.

405. _____. "Music and electronics: a report."
Perspectives of New Music 4, 2 (1966),
68-75.

Papers presented at the 1965 meeting of the
Audio Engineering Society are reviewed and
evaluated here for musicians. MAESTRO,
written by Robert Clark, and MUSIC4F by
Arthur Roberts are two music programs
discussed here at length.

406. _____. Music 4BF: a FORTRAN version of
Music 4B. Princeton University Department
of Music, 1967. Mimeo.

407. _____. "MUSIC7." *Computers and the Humanities* 5, 5 (May 1971), 311.

The author discusses his music program for
the Sigma 7 computing system.

408. _____. *MUSIC7 Reference Manual*. New York:
Queens College Press, 1972. 109 pp.

The format of the score and score cards,
standard generator subroutines, and the
MUSIC7 orchestra compiler are described.
A complete outline of program procedures
and some optional subprograms are given.

409. _____, moderator. "Panel discussion: computer
synthesis of sound, new ideas." *Proceedings
of the American Society of University Composers* 6 (1971), 13-48.

Papers by Vercoe, Clough, Layzer, Dodge, and Evans (see individual entries); comments.

410. _____. "Review." *Perspectives of New Music* 9, 2/ 10, 1 (Fall-Winter 1971), 350-355.

Review of two dissertations involving computer-assisted analysis of scores. As a composer and one dedicated to fruitful uses of technology in the arts, the author takes umbrage at applications which are too narrow in scope to produce meaningful conclusions or are characterized by unsophisticated approaches to music paired with high-technology research tools.

411. _____. "Review." *Computers and the Humanities* 7, 3 (Jan. 1973), 188-189.

Review of P. Grossi's Instruction Manual of DCMP, a music program written at the University of Pisa, Italy. See Grossi.

412. _____. "Some combinatorial properties of pitch structures." *Perspectives of New Music* 4, 1 (Fall-Winter 1965), 45-61.

The author describes some of his compositional techniques which have led him to the use of digital sound-generation systems.

413. _____; and Alexander M. Jones. IML, an Intermediary Musical Language. Princeton: Princeton University Music Department, Feb. 1964. 15 pp.

414. Huggins, Phyllis. "Three-part music with a computer as one part." *Computers and Automation* 7, 3 (March 1958), 8.

415. Hunt, Jerry. "Audio/video synthesis." *Synapse* 1, 6 (March/April 1977), 26-29.

An audio system including both analog electronic sub-units and digital devices is described. A ROM plug-in (disc memory) provides for major program changes in performance.

416. "Iannis Xenakis et La Musique Stochastique." Special issue of *La Revue Musicale* 257 (1963), 1-24.

Articles by Richard, Barraud, and Phillippot. See individual entries. Short bibliography of Xenakis' works also.

417. "Introduction till musikprogrammet EMS-1." *EMS-information* 5 (1972), 1-31. Mimeo.

A user's manual for the hybrid digital-analog system at the Electronic Music Studio, Stockholm.

418. Isaacson, Leonard M. See Hiller and Isaacson.

419. Jaffrennou, Pierre-Alain. "Du synthétiseur électronique à l'ordinateur." *Cahiers recherche/musique* [Paris: INA/GRM]

The use of voltage controlled modules as a model for digital synthesis programming and other concepts are discussed.

420. _____. "Une évolution de Music V vers la synthèse de sons à caractère concret." *Cahiers recherche/musique* [Paris: INA/GRM]

Report on the use of the Music V synthesis program at the GRM (Groupe de Recherche Musicale). Their aim is to produce sounds which have the character of natural sounds other than orchestral instruments. The focus is on the

"microscopic" level of timbre, as well as
the "macroscopic" aspects (duration, succes-
sion, variation, etc.). Examples of instruments devised are listed in the "chronique
de sons" that follows the article.

421. _____. "Histoires d'energie." *Cahiers
recherche/musique* [Paris: INA/GRM] 3 (1976),
120-142.

Report on the use of the Music V program to
test hypotheses relating to the time-variant
nature of the parameters of natural sounds.
One outcome is the design of digital instruments that include aleatoric variations of
each parameter, at different levels, with
special attention given to envelope generation.

422. James, David. Real-time tone synthesis from white
noise using high speed digital speech
processors. Paper presented at the First
International Conference on Computer Music,
Massachussetts Institute of Technology,
Oct. 28-31, 1976.

A description is given of a system employing four high speed signal processing
computers connected with a PDP 11/45 unit
in a computer ring network at M.I.T. A
synthesis technique used with this system
is demonstrated, by which harmonic spectra
are generated from white noise using high
Q resonators.

423. Jarrett, Alfred. New music in the U.S.A., 1960-
1966. M.M. diss., Howard University, 1967.

Computer music is included in a survey of
developments in American music from 1960
to 1966.

424. Johnston, Ben. "Contribution to IMC panel."
     Composer [U.S.] 2, 1 (1970), 6-8.

425. _____. "Tonality regained." *Proceedings of
     the American Society of University Composers*
     6 (1971), 113-119.

     Explanation of the composer's use of just
     intonation. Phases 1, 2, and 3 of a project
     conducted by Ed Kobrin and the author are
     described. A computer program is being
     written to generate compositional decisions
     based on scale systems in just intonation,
     generated also by means of the computer.
     Phase 3 is the design of an interface
     between a PDP-5 computing system and music
     synthesizer equipment. Hardware is being
     designed by Ed Kobrin. A commission from
     Paul Zukofsky, violinist, is mentioned.

426. _____; and Ed Kobrin. "Phase 1a." *Source*
     4, 1 (Jan. 1970), 27-45.

     This article includes a flow-chart and
     program in FORTRAN for the derivation of
     all ratio scales based on any two prime
     numbers greater than one, a presentation
     of one-dimensional ratio matrices, and
     musically notated scale families based on
     the numbers 2 and 3, 2 and 5, 2 and 7, and
     2 and 11. Remarks on inclusiveness, maps,
     graphs, and ratios, as well as other topics,
     make up the text of the article.

427. Jones, Alexander M. See Howe and Jones.

428. Jones, Cameron. Input language bandwidth: a
     statistical study. Paper presented at
     the 60th annual convention of the Audio
     Engineering Society, Los Angeles, May 2-5,
     1978.

The point is made that the rate of change
of control data may be arbitrarily high
when digital controls are used with a
digital synthesizer. The composer's specification of data is compared to the idea
of bandwidth.

429. _____. See Alonso, Appleton, and Jones.

430. Jones, Edward. A multiwaveform organ: from
computer to optoelectronics. Paper presented
to the 43rd convention of the Audio Engineering Society, New York, Sept. 12-15, 1972.

Measured tone spectra of outstanding organ
stops are stored in a large computer. These
are converted to digital magnetic tapes
which control a Baldwin synchronous photo-
graphic disc recorder. In the Baldwin organ,
each key for each stop has a separate
optoelectronic circuit for envelope control.

431. Joyce, James. "Hardware for the humanist: what you
should know and why." *Computers and the
Humanities* 11, 5 (Sept.-Oct. 1977), 299-
307.

Practical advice for computer users in the
humanities, including some discussion of
microprocessors now available and applicable to various projects in the humanities.
Directed toward the uninitiated, this article
provides definitions for basic terminology.

432. Justice, James H. Analytical signal processing
in music computation. Paper presented
at the First International Conference on
Computer Music, Massachussetts Institute
of Technology, Oct. 28-31, 1976.

Analytical signal processing is used to

describe waveforms in terms of time-varying envelopes and phase terms which are computable via the discrete Hilbert transform.

433. _____. "Recursive digital filtering in music computation." In *Software Synthesis Techniques*, Proceedings of the Second Annual Music Computation Conference, Nov. 7-9, 1975, part 1. Urbana: University of Illinois, 1975. 22-31.

A short course in digital filtering is given, with further remarks on the author's own work with time-varying filters (in progress at this date) and comments on the musical use of digital filtering in sound synthesis.

434. _____. "Frequency domain design of recursive digital filters using Pade approximation techniques." Technical report, University of Tulsa, 1975.

435. _____. "Frequency domain design of two-dimensional recursive filters." Technical report, University of Tulsa, 1975.

436. _____; and J.L. Shanks. "Stability criterion for N-dimensional digital filters." *IEEE Transactions on Automated Control*, AC-18, 3, 284-286.

437. Kaegi, Werner. "A minimum description of the linguistic sign repertoire (first part)." *Interface* 2 (1973), 141-156. Part 2: *Interface* 3 (1974), 137-157.

Relationships between linguistics and musical structures are being explored by the author. A model is presented whereby linguistic signs can be described. Signal patterns which generate linguistic signs are examined. Formulations resulting from experiments, with the author himself as test subject, are presented.

438. _____. "Le modèle de synthèse de son 'VOSIM' et ses aspects psychoacoustiques." Proc. Symposium sur la Psychoacoustique musicale, IRCAM (Institut de Recherche et Coordination Acoustique/Musique), Paris, July 11-13, 1977. (In press.)

439. _____."Musique et technologie dans l'Europe de 1970." *La Revue Musicale* 268-269 (1971), 9-30.

Also, as "Music and technology in the Europe of 1970." In *Music and Technology*. Paris: La Revue Musicale, 1971. 11-31.

Historical developments leading up to the use of computers in musical composition are traced. A discussion of the technological influences on the nature of modern music concludes the article.

440. _____. "Die Musik unserer Zeit-- ein Opfer der Technik?" *World Music* 13, 1 (1970), 4-17. In Ger., Eng., Fr.

The author predicts that the computer will be the instrument of the future, replacing standard musical instruments, and music will be defined as information.

441. _____. *Was ist elektronische musik*. Zurich: Orell Fussli Verlag, 1967.

Text on electronic music and precepts for the author's continuing work in the field of digital synthesis.

442. _____. See Tempelaars and Kaegi.

443. Kaehler, Ted. "Some music at Xerox PARC." In
    Software Synthesis Techniques, Proceedings
    of the Second Annual Music Computation
    Conference, Nov. 7-9, 1975, part 1. Urbana:
    University of Illinois, 1975. 53-57.

    A music system which synthesizes five
    voices in real-time, utilizing Chowning's
    frequency modulation technique, has been
    developed at the Xerox Palo Alto Research
    Center. The digital synthesizer, called
    Twang, is controlled by a special purpose
    computer language called Smalltalk and has
    a number of editing features. A keyboard
    controller is also available, and output
    can be monitored on an animated CRT picture
    of the music in player-piano-roll notation.
    See also Saunder's "Real-time digital FM
    audio synthesis."

444. Kahrs, M. A computer language for psychoacoustic
    study and musical control of timbre. Paper
    presented at the 1977 International Computer
    Music Conference, Center for Music Experi-
    ment and Related Research, University of
    California at San Diego, Oct. 1977.

445. Karantchentzeff, P. See Risset, Charbonneau, and
    Karantchentzeff.

446. Karkoschka, Erhard. "Letzer Schreck: Der Computer."
    Melos 39, 5 (1972), 285-288.

    A history of electronic music up to the
    use of the computer to produce data tran-
    scribed to musical notation, music/graph-
    ical art, and as a control for electronic
    apparatus. The digital hybrid studio in
    Stockholm (with photographs included) and

computer graphics by H. Brün are discussed.

447. Karwoski, Rick. Predictive coding for greater
     accuracy in successive approximation A/D
     converters. Paper presented to the 57th
     convention of the Audio Engineering
     Society, Los Angeles, May 10–13, 1977.
     Preprint No. 1228 A-6.

     Digitization of high quality audio requires
     precision successive approximation A/D
     conversion circuitry. Utilizing predictive
     coding techniques and integrated circuitry
     technology, a scheme similar to some used
     in speech applications has been devised
     and is presented here.

448. Kassler, Jamie C. "Report from London: Cybernetic
     Serendipity." *Current Musicology* 7 (1968),
     47–59.

     Review of an exhibit held in London, in 1968,
     of creative forms inspired by technological
     advances, activities which represent 'the
     link between random systems employed by
     artists, composers, and poets, and those
     involved in the use of cybernetic devices.'
     H. Brün's *Stalks and Trees and Drops and
     Clouds* is reproduced in score form, in part.
     Also, M.V. Mathews, J.R. Pierce, Wilhelm
     Fucks, T.H. O'Beirne, Peter Zinovieff,
     Alan Sutcliffe, Tristram Carey, Lejaren
     Hiller, L.M. Isaacson, R.A. Baker, James
     Tenney, Haruki Tsuchiya, David Lewin, H. Brün,
     James Cuomo, Gerald Strang, John Cage,
     David Tudor, Iannis Xenakis, and J.K. Randall
     are listed as music exhibitors. The inade-
     quacy of composer/scientist distinctions
     here and the artists' concern with systems
     of control and chance are discussed. Scores
     by I. Xenakis are also reproduced here.

449. Kassler, Michael. "Decision of a musical system."
Communications of the Association for Computing Machinery 5, 4 (1962), 223.

Research summary. An algorithm has been written which allows an automatic decision to be made as to whether a given musical score in normal musical notation is an example of Schoenberg's system of twelve-tone musical composition.

450. Kleen, Leslie D. Two research projects in musical applications of electronic digital computers. National Science Foundation Project No. GK-14191, Technical Report No. 3, Buffalo, N.Y., June 1972. 133 pp. Mimeo.

451. Knopoff, Leon. "A progress report on an experiment in musical synthesis." *Selected Reports* 1, 1 (1966), 49-60.

A brief description is given of work being carried out at Bell Laboratories by M.V. Mathews on his Music IV program for digital synthesis.

452. Knowlton, Prentiss. "Computer meets keyboard." *Synapse* 1, 5 (Jan.-Feb. 1977), 10.

A PDP-8 computing system and a paper tape reader are used to perform a player-piano type function with a pipe organ. A record album has been produced, entitled *Unplayed by Human Hands*.

453. Kobrin, Edward G. HYBRID IV Users' Manual. Unpublished manuscript, Center for Music Experiment, La Jolla, Cal., 1975.

454. _____. "I Ching." *Source* 4, 2 (July 1970), 1-7.

This article includes a complete program for chance operations derived from the I Ching, with flow-chart, print-out of the program, and samples of the derived hexagrams.

455. _____. *KOBRIN: Computer in Performance.* West Berlin, Ger.: Berliner Kuenstler-programme des Deutschen Akademischen Austauschdientes, 1977. 24 pp. Available through Lingua Press, La Jolla, Cal.

Includes two-page reproduction of one of Kobrin's scores for a piece realized on the composer's HYBRID IV system, circuit schematics, photographs of the system and of Kobrin in performance, and an interview by Jolyn Brettingham-Smith.

456. _____. "Investigation of various compositional devices." *Computers and the Humanities* 3, 2 (Nov. 1968), 112.

457. _____. "Notation of computer generated music." *Computers and the Humanities* 3, 5 (May 1969), 311.

Above two items are listing of research in progress, described in abbreviated form, as part of a directory.

458. _____; and T.H. Ashford. "A solution to the problems of vertical serialization." *Perspectives of New Music* 6, 2 (1968), 119-124.

The composer Kobrin describes his system of serial composition using a 3600 CDC computer and programs written in ALGOL 60, at Northwestern University, with particular attention paid to the problem of accomodating melodic movement with vertical control. The flow-chart of the program and a short example of COMPUTERMUSIK IV, a composition produced with this program and transcribed into musical notation, are included. The complete score may be had by writing to E.G. Kobrin.

459. _____; and Jeffrey Mack. The HYBRID II: a real-time composing/performing computer synthesis system. Center for Music Experiment, University of California at San Diego, 1974. 14 pp.

User's manual for earlier version of hybrid system developed in La Jolla, Cal.

460. _____. See Johnston and Kobrin.

461. Koenig, Gottfried M. "Computer-Verwendung in Kompositionsprozessen." *Musik auf der Flucht vor sich selbst.* Reihe Hanser 28. Munich: Hanser, 1969. 78-91.

The author describes in detail his composing program of 1967-69 and his method of transcription of the computer score.

462. _____. "Construction and working methods of the Utrecht University studio." *Electronic Music Reports* [Institute of Sonology, University of Utrecht] 1 (1969), 61-67.

The use of the computer in music-making at Utrecht is described in brief.

463. _____. "Datorns användning i kompositoriska processer." *Nutida Musik* 13, 4 (1969-70), 26-31.

Description of the author's work with programming structural controls which, when applied to electronic sound generators, will produce compositions in line with the composer's concept of music as a process.

464. _____. *Electronic Music Course: Computer Composition*. Utrecht: Institute of Sonology at Utrecht State University, 1971.

Course outline/users' manual for the author's composing program PROJEKT 2.

465. _____. "Emploi des programmes d'ordinateur dans la création musicale." *La Revue Musicale* 268-269 (1971), 89-112.

Also, as "The use of computer programmes in creating music." *Music and Technology*. Paris: La Revue Musicale, 1971. 93-115.

A brief historical survey is taken of the use of the computer in composition, with a discussion of notational problems. Following this is a description of the author's composing program and automation of the analog studio by computer (PROJEKT 2). Diagrams, print-outs, a computer score and parts, a pitch graph, and musical transcription are included.

466. _____. Interview. *Numus-West* [Mercer Island, Washington] 1 (April 1973), 29-30.

The current philosophy of the Institute of Sonology, various research activities, and the teaching program at the Institute are discussed here, with Louis Christensen as interviewer.

467. _____. "My experiences in programmed music." *Faire* [Bourges: Editions GMEB] 4/5 (May 1978), 10-15.

The composer traces the development of his idea of music as an algorithmic process.

468. _____. "Notes on the computer in music." *The World of Music* 9, 3 (1967), 3-13. In Eng., Ger., Fr.

Introductory article for the musician on the use of the computer in composition. A flow-chart for the formation of repetitions in groups is included.

469. _____. "Project 1." *Electronic Music Reports* [Institute of Sonology, Utrecht University] 2 (July 1970), 32-44.

The author presents his program for the calculation of musical structures written in FORTRAN II for use with an IBM 7090 machine; a second version was written in ALGOL 60 for use with an Electrologica X8 computer. A flow-chart of the program, compositional diagram, and a brief description of a printing program are given.

470. _____. "Project 2." *Electronic Music Reports* [Institute of Sonology, Utrecht University] 3 (1970), 1-16.

The author's program for the calculation of musical structure variants is described in terms of basic principles, the structure formula, and input and output formats. This

'composing program' is intended for general
use and for research into compositional
theory. Diagrams, illustrations, and an
index are included.

471. _____. See Tempelaars and Koenig.

472. Konieczny, Jacek. "Zastosowanie maszyn cyfrowych
do komponowania muzyki." *Zeszyty Naukowe.*
Państwowa Wyższa Szkola Muzyczna [Poland]
12 (1973), 121-142. Mimeo.

A brief survey of connections between
electronics and music and of the applications of computers in music. The author's
own experiments in composing music by computer are described.

473. Kostka, Stefan M. *Bibliography of Computer
Applications in Music.* Music Indexes
and Bibliographies, No. 7. Hackensack,
N.J.: Joseph Boonin, Inc., 1974. 58 pp.

Contains 641 entries, including all writings
of significance up to 1973, on uses of computers by musicologists, theorists, and
composers.

474. Krellman, Hanspeter. "Mathematiker unter den
zeitgenössichen Komponisten." *Melos*
39, 6 (1972), 322-325.

The author emphasizes the importance of
Xenakis, a composer who abandoned the
polyphonic structure of serialism and turned
to non-polyphonic musical structures derived
from mathematics, using the computer as an
aid in calculating the musical details.

475. Kristensen, Erik. See Laursen and Kristensen.

476. Kriz, J. Stanley. "A 16-bit A-D-A conversion
     system for high-fidelity audio research."
     IEEE Transactions of ASSP 23, 1 (1975),
     146-149.

     An A/D and D/A converter system with
     exceptionally wide dynamic range and
     low distortion is described. The tradi-
     tional 12-bit A-D-A conversion of high
     quality audio is becoming inadequate for
     high quality audio analysis and synthesis
     research. The need for greater dynamic
     range and low distortion has led to the
     development of a 16-bit converter system
     designed specifically for audio service
     at Carnegie-Mellon University.

477. _____. "The specification of digital-to-
     analog converters for audio." In *Hardware
     for Computer-Controlled Sound Synthesis*,
     Proceedings of the Second Annual Music
     Computation Conference, Nov. 7-9, 1975,
     part 4. Urbana: University of Illinois,
     1975. 43-46.

     The relationship between available
     specifications of digital-to-analog
     converters and the requirements of audio
     reproduction is drawn here. It is pointed
     out that this type of equipment was de-
     signed originally for other purposes and
     factors which were considered in the de-
     sign are not the same as those critical to
     audio applications. A converter intended
     for audio use has been developed at
     Carnegie-Mellon University and is now
     available from Three Rivers Computer
     Corporation.

478. Kuksa, Emanuel. "Duvaj na generatoru." *Opus Muszy* 5, 1 (1973), 4-9.

The author has analyzed the melodic and rhythmic construction of folk tunes in order to establish criteria for automated composition of folk-like melodies and is investigating ways in which such criteria can be applied to contemporary music.

479. Kupper, Hubert. *Computer und musikalische Kompositionen.* Braunschweig: Vieweg, 1970. 41 pp.

480. _____. "Computer und musikalische Kompositionen." *Elektronische Datenverarbeitung* 11 (1969), 492-497.

Short description of uses of computers by composers.

481. Kupper, Leo. "Elaboration de musique électronique à partir d'un ordinateur musical. Tendance à l'automatisation de la composition. Génération d'un monde sonore autonome par interstimulations d'automates sonores." *Faire* [Bourges: Editions GMEB] 2-3 (1975), 31-41.

The composer describes his computer-controlled custom-designed system for sound synthesis and his concept of music-making as a system of interdependencies. His electronic 'creatures' are interconnected so that one programmed sonorous event triggers another in an ongoing, continuously varying composition.

482. Lachartre, Nicole. "Les musiques artificielles."
     Diagrammes du Monde [Editions du CAP,
     Monaco] 146 (April 1969), 1-96.

     Computer applications in music from 1956
     to 1969 are reviewed. Following is a dis-
     cussion of the relationship between music
     and mathematics in techniques of analysis
     and composition and problems of these
     techniques. Acoustical works by Hiller,
     Barbaud, Xenakis, Phillipot, Fucks, Koenig,
     Moles, and Lachartre are examined, as well
     as sound synthesis works by Mathews, Pierce,
     Guttman, Risset, and Rosler at Bell Tele-
     phone Laboratories.

483. Lake, Robin B.; and Raph Cherubini. "Orthogonal
     transforms for sound synthesis." In
     Software Synthesis Techniques, Proceedings
     of the Second Annual Music Computation
     Conference, Nov. 7-9, 1975, part 1. Urbana:
     University of Illinois, 1975.

     Orthogonal transforms, a class of algorithms
     which includes the Fast Fourier Transform,
     and Walsh functions are explained briefly.
     A sound-synthesis system at Case Western
     Reserve University is described as direct
     sound synthesis with Fast Fourier and Fast
     Walsh Transforms, utilizing a PDP-11/45
     computer system, A/D and D/A conversion,
     and a Tektronix interactive graphics display.

484. Lansky, Paul. See Cann, Lansky, Steiglitz, and
     Zukerman.

485. Laske, Otto E. "Considering human memory in
     designing user interfaces for computer
     music." *Computer Music Journal* 2, 4
     (late Dec. 1978), 39-45.

Parallels are drawn between computer music systems and a particular model of human memory. This model defines four classes of production: perceptual, semantic, syntactic, and general. It is suggested that user interfaces should be designed to obtain behavioral data documenting musical activity as corresponding to this model.

486. _____. "Information-processing psychology today: its problems and methods." Onderzoeks memorandum AMS-3. Subfaculteit Psychologie, State University of Utrecht, The Netherlands, 1974.

Revised version appears as "The information-processing approach to musical cognition." *Interface* 3, 2 (Spring 1975), 109-136.

The current ideas of behavioral scientists are applied to music-making as an activity, with digital sound synthesis serving as an experimental tool.

487. _____. "Introduction to a generative theory of music." *Sonological Reports* [Institute of Sonology, Utrecht] 1 (1973), 103-111.

Using artificial intelligence, the author is proposing a type of performance model for music in order to demonstrate an algorithmic theory of music.

488. _____. "Musical acoustics (sonology): a questionable science reconsidered." *Numus-West* [Mercer Island, Washington] 1, 6 (1974), 35-40.

An attempt to relate music to psychoacoustics and sociology. The approach to this problem

is compared to that of attempts to build
automatic speech-understanding systems.
The author concludes that information-
processing, rather than signal-processing,
is an appropriate model, a methodology
that has arrived with the advent of the
digital computer.

489. _____. "Musical semantics, a procedural
point of view, part 1." *Proceedings,
First International Symposium on the
Semiotics of Music, Belgrade, Yugoslavia,
1973.* Pesaro: Centro di Iniziativa Cult-
urale, 1974. 214-224.

490. _____. "On musical strategies with a view
to a generative theory of music." *Interface*
1, 2 (Nov. 1972), 111-125.

Automatic simulation of compositional activities, using a linguistic model of music,
is discussed.

491. _____. *On Problems of a Performance Model
for Music.* Utrecht: Institute of Sonology,
1972.

492. _____. "On psychomusicology." *International
Review of the Aesthetics and Sociology of
Music* [Zagreb, Yugoslavia] 6, 2 (Winter
1975), 21-40.

493. _____. On the methodology and implementation
of a procedural theory of music. Paper presented at the International Conference on
the Computer and the Humanities, Minneapolis,
Minnesota, 1973. 40 pp.

Summarized in *Computational Musicology
Newsletter* 1, 1 (Oct. 1973), 15-16.

494. _____. "On the understanding and design of aesthetic artifacts." In *Musik und Verstehen*, ed. P. Faltin et al. Cologne: Arno Volk Verlag, 1974. 189-216.

495. _____. "Toward a center for studies in musical intelligence." *Numus-West* [Mercer Island, Washington] 1, 5 (1974), 44-46.

Proposal for the establishment of a computer facility for investigation of suitable performance models which explain psychological and sociological aspects of music.

496. _____. "Toward a musical intelligence system: OBSERVER." *Numus-West* [Mercer Island, Washington] 1, 4 (1973), 11-16.

Short introduction to an investigation into musical problem-solving using real-time digital sound synthesis facilities. An outline is given of a series of programs called OBSERVER. These programs provide for an interactive system and for artificial musical problem-solving with learning processes implemented into the computer system. Illustrations and bibliography included.

497. _____. "Toward a theory of interfaces for computer music systems." *Computer Music Journal* 1, 4 (Nov. 1977), 53-60.

Adaptation of Chapter Eight of the monograph *Music, Memory, and Thought: Explorations in Cognitive Musicology*. Ann Arbor: Xerox University Microfilms, 1977. Copyright, Otto E. Laske, 1977. 163-180.

Design objectives for computer music systems serving instructional purposes are discussed and topics of research in the interactive

behavior of users of such systems are outlined. The emphasis is on the need for
analysis of cognitive processes of composers
and for an empirical theory of music interfaces in digital synthesis systems.

498. _____. "Toward a theory of musical cognition." *Interface* 4, 2 (Dec. 1975), 147-
208.

Also, appears in Onderzoeksmemorandum AMS-10,
Subfaculteit Psychologie, State University
of Utrecht, The Netherlands, 1975.

The concept of musical science as a behavioral science is developed. As an example
of a theory of musical cognition, a program
called OBSERVER is discussed. The program
consists of two parts, one for sound synthesis and one to provide syntactic and
semantic instructions.

499. _____. "Toward a theory of musical instruction." *Interface* 5, 3 (Nov. 1976), 125-
148.

The author investigates the determinants of
expert behavior in musical composition.
Interactive sound synthesis programs are
seen as relevant to instruction in composition. A model of the musical learner is
proposed.

500. _____. Toward a theory of user interfaces
for computer music systems. Paper presented
at the First International Conference on
Computer Music, Massachussetts Institute
of Technology, Oct. 28-31, 1976.

Discussion of a system that gathers data
concerning the procedures employed by its
user in order to study compositional
processes. This is aimed at developing a
theory of user interfaces in computer music
systems.

501. Laursen, Thorkild; and Erik Bak Kristensen.
Brugermanual til 960A SAL-cross-assembler.
DAIMI MD-8, Department of Musical Acoustics,
Institute of Musicology, University of
Aarhus, April 1974.

Users' manual for program written for digital sound synthesizer developed in Aarhus,
Denmark.

502. Lawson, James R.   See Gardner, Harvey, Lawson,
and Risset.

503. _____; and Max V. Mathews. "Computer program
to control a digital real-time sound synthesizer." *Computer Music Journal* 1, 4
(Nov. 1977), 16-21.

Programming work originated at the French
research center IRCAM (Institut de Recherche
et Coordination Acoustique/Musique) is
described. Discussion begins with a short
explanation of overtone summation and FM
synthesis, two techniques of sound synthesis
to be employed by the Alles-DiGiugno digital synthesizer system under development at
IRCAM. A summary of the hardware to be used
along with DEC's LSI-11 microcomputer is
offered. The general form of parameterized
score is the same as that used by MUSIC V
systems.

504. Lay, J.E. A music realization by hybrid computer.
Paper presented at the 48th convention of
the Audio Engineering Society, Los Angeles,
May 7-10, 1974.

A hybrid system at Michigan State University is described. Theory, circuitry, and
coding are discussed and musical examples
presented. The system is capable of multichannel operation.

505. _____. Walsh functions in audio education
and electronic music. Paper presented at
the 50th convention of the Audio Engineering Society, London, March 4-7, 1975.
Included in *Collected Preprints of the
50th AES Convention*. London: AES, 1975.

An overview of the characteristics of
Walsh functions is first given. Applications
for analysis, filtering, and bandwidth-
reduction of speech, electrocardio- and
electroencephalograms; multiplexing of
communication channels; processing images;
and composing electronic music are discussed.
Three low-cost synthesis schemes are outlined, with the use of Walsh functions in
digital synthesis being another possibility.

506. Layzer, Arthur. "Some idiosyncratic aspects of
computer synthesized sound." *Proceedings
of the American Society of University Composers* 6 (Spring 1973), 27-39.

The author discusses characteristic ways in
which the digital medium influences the
sound and musical organization of digitally
synthesized compositions. Topics include
digital feedback instruments, digital imi-
tation of conventional musical sounds, and
invariants of complex sound experience. The

118

concept of a programmed language of transformations on musical base material is
introduced.

507. Leal, Antonio. See Hiller and Leal.

508. LeBrun, Marc. "A derivation of the spectrum of
FM with a complex modulating wave." *Computer
Music Journal* 1, 4 (Nov. 1977), 51-52.

A concise, mathematical exposition is given
here on the results obtained when a
complex signal is used as the modulating
waveform in a technique of using frequency
modulation to create complex audio spectra
through digital waveform generation. (The
modulation index and ratio of carrier frequency to modulating frequency are chosen
by the composer. The outcome of the added
complication is given a formula here.)

509. _____. "Notes on microcomputer music."
*Conference Proceedings of the First West
Coast Computer Faire.* Palo Alto, Cal.:
Computer Faire, 1977.

Reprinted in *Computer Music Journal* 1, 2
(April 1977), 30-35.

Several points are made with reference to
applying methods of computer sound synthesis
developed at large research centers to the
microcomputers recently available to indi-
viduals. The importance of psychoacoustics,
and the need to distinguish between those
functions which must be performed at high
rates and high precision and those which
may be performed more slowly, are emphasized.
Suggestions are given for data reduction,
table reduction, and savings in multipliers.
Nonlinear synthesis techniques such as

Chowning's FM technique and algorithms
being investigated by James Moorer and the
author now are also cost-effective means
of producing interesting sounds. Also
mentioned: digital filtering, inverse
Fast Fourier Transforms, and small modules
such as the digital reverberator which may
be controlled by a microcomputer.

510. Ledley, Robert S. *Programming and Utilizing
Digital Computers.* New York: McGraw-Hill,
1962. 568 pp.

511. Lefkoff, Gerald. "Automated discovery of similar
segments in the forty-eight permutations
of a twelve-tone row." In *The Computer
and Music,* ed. Harry B. Lincoln. Ithaca:
Cornell University Press, 1970. 147-153.

A program has been written by the author
to produce all possible permutations of
a twelve-tone row and to compare them
automatically for a common characteristic
deemed important by the composer.

512. _____, ed. *Papers from the West Virginia
University Conference on Computer Applications in Music.* Morgantown, W. Va.: West
Virginia University Foundation, 1967.
105 pp.

This is a collection of essays on the application of the computer to various fields of
music, two of which are relevant to composition. The first of these is "An introduction to the information processing capabilities of the computer" by Charles C.
Cook. This is a summary of programming
procedure and a general overview of computer
usage in music. A list of peripheral devices
is included. The other article is "Program-

ming a computer for musical composition"
by Lejaren Hiller. A technical explanation
of the program MUSICOMP is given. Graphical
illustrations of the structure of *Computer
Cantata* and excerpts from scores to *Sonifer-
ous Loops* by H. Brün and the author's
Algorithms I are included.

513. Leitner, P. *Logische Programme für automatische
Musik*. Wien: Staatsprüfungsarbeit an der
Technischen Hochschule, 1957.

514. Lesche, Carl. "Weltanschauung, science, technologie,
et art." *La Revue Musicale* 268-269 (1971),
37-55.

Also, as "Weltanschauung, science, technology,
and art." In *Music and Technology*. Paris:
La Revue Musicale, 1971. 39-55.

The relationships between world-view, science,
technology, and art are examined and tend-
encies towards formalization and experimental
thought in the arts are attributed to the
inspiration of computer technology.

515. Lin, Ehr. "Playing the computer." *Gravesaner
Blätter* 27-28 (Nov. 1965), 81-84. Eng., Ger.

A brief description of Divilbiss' program,
Music Maker, and the 'Music Machine' at the
University of Illinois.

516. Lincoln, Harry B., ed. *The Computer and Music*.
Ithaca: Cornell University Press, 1970.
354 pp.

Also, as *Kompyûtâ to ongaku*. Tokyo: Kawai-
gakufu, 1972. Trans. by Minao Shibata and
Tokumaru Yoshihiko and others. 357 pp.

This book includes essays on the use of
the computer in composition, analysis,
ethnomusicology, music history, style
analysis, music information retrieval,
and historical background of such uses.
Of relevance to composition and sound-
generation are: "Musicke's handmaiden: or
technology in the service of the arts" by
Edmund A. Bowles (historical overview of
the application of technology in the arts);
"From musical ideas to computers and back"
by Herbert Brün (aesthetic/philosophical
viewpoint); "MUSPEC" by Jack P. Citron
(description of experimental composition
program); "Music composed with computers--
a historical survey" by Lejaren Hiller
(survey of the use of computers in composition from 1956 to 1968); "FORTRAN music
programs involving numerically related
tones" by Ian Morton and John Lofstedt
(programs for composition and analysis);
and "Ethics and esthetics of computer
composition" by Gerald Strang (human responsibility for aesthetic judgements in
computer music). See Bowles, Citron, Brün,
Hiller, Morton, and Strang.

517. _____. "The computer seminar at Binghamton:
a report." *Notes* 23 (1967-68), 236-240.

518. _____. "Uses of the computer in music compo-
sition and research." In *Advances in
Computers,* ed. Morris Rubinoff. New York:
Academic Press, 1973. Vol. 12. 73-114.

Introductory article, briefly describing
compositions which use computers for certain
tasks, with output transcribed for performance by traditional means; use of computers
for control of synthesizers, and digital
synthesis. Applications in research and

automated music typography are represented
also. A discography and list of references
are provided. A history of the earliest
uses of computers by musicians is given.

519. Lindblom, B. "Music composed by a computer
program." *Speech Transmission Laboratory
Report* [Royal Institute of Technology,
Stockholm] 4 (Jan. 15, 1973), 20-28.

Discussion of work produced with a hybrid
system at the Electronic Music Studio in
Stockholm.

520. Lofstedt, John. See Morton and Lofstedt.

521. Logemann, G.W. "Techniques for programmed electronic
synthesis." *Electronic Music Review* 1
(Jan. 1967), 44-53.

Techniques for the use of paper control
tapes and digital computers as control
devices are discussed.

522. Loy, Gareth. "Record review." *Computer Music
Journal* 1, 2 (April 1977), 61.

Review of *The Dartmouth Digital Synthesizer*,
Folkways Records FTS 33442. (Music by
Jon Appleton, Lars-Gunnar Bodin, Russell
Pinkston, William Brunson.)

523. _____. "Record review. *Computer Music
Journal* 2, 1 (July 1978), 60-61.

Review of *Sonic Landscapes*, electronic and
computer music by Barry Truax, Melbourne
SMLP 4033, stereo, Imperial Record Corp.,
Vancouver, B.C., Canada. Also reviewed is
"Studies for Trumpet and Computer" by
Dexter Morrill, on *Maurice Stith Plays*

Contemporary Literature for the Trumpet,
Golden Crest Records, Inc. RE-7068, 220
Broadway, Huntington Station, N.Y.

524. _____. See Rush, Moorer, Loy.

525. _____. "Reviews." *Computer Music Journal*
2, 4 (late Dec. 1978), 6-9.

Review of a double album recording called
*New Directions in Music, Significant
Contemporary Works for the Computer,*
recorded and distributed by Tulsa Studios,
6314 E. 13th St., Tulsa, Oklahoma 74112.
The works included, all carefully described
and reviewed here, are *Mar-ri-ia-a,* "A
Miniature Opera for Computer and Chamber
Ensemble" by Joseph P. Olive (New Jersey -
libretto by Joan S. Olive); *Los Nombres* by
Diane Thome (Seattle); *Effetti Collaterali*
by James Dashow (Rome); *Episodes I & II* by
William McKee (Tulsa); *Dance* by Dean Walraff
(Cambridge); *Inharmonic Soundscapes* by
Jean-Claude Risset (Paris); *Voices* by Tracy
Lind Petersen (Salt Lake City); *Brazen* by
Emmanuel Ghent (New York); and *Antony* by
David Wessel (Paris).

526. Luce, David A. "Dynamic spectrum changes of
orchestral instruments." *Journal of the Audio
Engineering Society* 23, 7 (Sept. 1975), 565.

Also, presented at the 51st convention of
the Audio Engineering Society, Los Angeles,
May 13-16, 1975. Preprint No. 1025.

Recordings of various orchestral instruments
were digitized, then analyzed with a view to
providing models for digital synthesis. The
study focuses on the spectral envelopes of
instruments at different dynamic levels.

527. _____. Physical correlates of nonpercussive musical instrument tones. Diss., Massachussetts Institute of Technology, 1963. 362 pp.

528. Lynner, Doug; and Virginia Quesada. "Jean-Claude Risset-- IRCAM from the inside out." *Synapse* 2, 5 (March/April 1978), 41.

Interview with Risset on the activities of the new music center in Paris. Brief outline of research carried out in 1977 is given. Also under discussion is the use of the DiGiugno synthesizer with a small LSI computer and digital synthesis involving a system based on the MUSIC V program and a PDP-10 computer.

529. Lyon, Raymond. "Algorithm I, musique écrit par une machine pour le film *Imprévisibles*." *Guide du Concert* 330 (Nov. 17, 1961), 385.

Review of the first film score to make use of computer-generated data translated into musical notation for performance by musicians.

530. _____. "La musique algorithmique." *Guide du Concert* 336 (Jan. 12 ,1962), 610.

Comments on the work of Barbaud, *Imprévisibles*.

531. MacDonald, Neil. "Music by automatic computers." *Computers and Automation* 7, 3 (March 1958), 8-9.

532. MacInnis, Donald. "Sound synthesis by computer: MUSIGOL, a program written entirely in extended ALGOL." *Perspectives of New Music* 7, 1 (Fall-Winter 1968), 66-79.

A program developed at the University of Virginia for a Burroughs 5500 computer is described, with an Ambilog 200 hybrid computer being used for D/A conversion. A list of basic instrument programs available and a diagram of the MUSIGOL block structure are included.

533. Mailliard, Bénédict. "Les distorsions de MUSIC V." *Cahiers recherche/musique* [Paris: INA/GRM] 3 (1976), 207-246.

A critique of MUSIC V is offered.

534. _____. "Notes sans ourlet." *Cahiers recherche/musique* [Paris: INA/GRM] 3 (1976), 164-178.

535. _____. "Souvenir d'un larsen." *Cahiers recherche/musique* [Paris: INA/GRM] 3 (1976), 143-163.

536. _____. "Sur la modulation de fréquence. Appendici: petite pedagogie sur la modulation de fréquence." *Cahiers recherche/ musique* [Paris: INA/GRM] 3 (1976), 179-206.

Tutorial on frequency modulation and its application by John Chowning to digital sound synthesis.

537. _____. "Surgeons." *Cahiers recherche/ musique* [Paris: INA/GRM] 3 (1976), 250-278.

Various subroutines devised by French composers and programmers to be added to a MUSIC V installation are described.

538. _____. See Chion and Mailliard.

539. Manthey, Michael. "The EGG Synthesizer, a purely digital real-time sound synthesizer." *Electronic Music and Musical Acoustics* [Aarhus, Dk.: Institute of Musicology, University of Aarhus. 1 (1975), 7-44.

Shortened version appears as "The EGG synthesizer: a purely digital, real-time polyphonic synthesizer." *Computer Music Journal* 2, 2 (Sept. 1978), 32-37.

Description of the EGG synthesizer, developed in a cooperative effort between the computer science and musicology departments at the University of Aarhus. The system includes a TI960 microcomputer, two touch-sensitive keyboards (one chromatic, the other microtonal), floppy disc memory, and a paper reader and puncher. There are various editing features.

540. _____. A User Manual for the EGG real-time digital sound synthesizer. Institute of Musicology, University of Aarhus, 1976. Unpublished ms.

541. Martin, Steven. Creating complex timbre through the use of amplitude modulation in the audio band. Paper presented at the 42nd convention of the Audio Engineering Society, Los Angeles, May 2-5, 1972.

A technique for digital synthesis of complex timbres by means of amplitude modulation is described. Examples were given and a method for smooth timbral transitions shown.

542. Massachussetts Institute of Technology. *Abstracts of Papers Read at the First International Conference on Computer Music.* Cambridge, Mass.: Department of Humanities, MIT, 1976.

Abstracts of papers on analysis/synthesis techniques, synthesis hardware, music input languages and editors, sound synthesis languages and editors, user-psychology, facilities, the composer's experience, digital sound editing, system design philosophies, real-time controls, and interactive composing are provided.

543. _____. See People's Computer Company (#673).

544. Mathews, Max V. "An acoustical compiler for music and psychological stimuli." *Bell System Technical Journal* 40, 3 (May 1961), 677-694.

This article is a technical description of an early version of the author's sound-generation program and is the first complete published description of such a program. The program is described as three operations: 1) instrument programs, 2) sequencing programs containing pitch and rhythm information, and 3) programs for calculating the sound pressure output in numbers that can be converted to an audio signal. A first composition is described.

545. _____. "The computer and music." *Computer Studies in the Humanities and Verbal Behavior* 3 (1970-72), 224-225.

Review of *The Computer and Music*, ed. by Harry B. Lincoln. Ithaca: Cornell University Press, 1970.

546. _____. "The computer as a musical instrument." *Computer Decisions* 4, 2 (Feb. 1972), 22-25.

A brief description of the author's work leading to MUSIC IV program for sound generation.

547. _____. "Computer composers-- comments and case histories." *Bulletin of the Computer Arts Society* 1 (Feb. 1970), 6.

Informal comments are made on the work of Tenney, Randall, Risset, Chowning, and Lewin.

548. _____. "The computer music record supplement." *Gravesaner Blätter* 7, 26 (1965), 117.

Four examples of computer music produced at Bell Telephone Laboratories are briefly described: "Cyclic Study," "Pergolesi Development," "Substitutions Study," and "Masquerades."

549. _____."Computer program to generate acoustic signals." *Journal of the Acoustical Society of America* 32 (1960), 1493. Abstract.

Presented to the 60th meeting of the American Acoustical Society.

Description of one of the author's early programs for synthesizing acoustical signals with a digital computer and D/A converter.

550. _____. The Conductor Program. Paper presented at the First International Conference on Computer Music, Massachussetts Institute of Technology, Oct. 28-31, 1976.

The GROOVE system, a program for performing music with a computer-controlled synthesizer, is described. This allows the performer to adjust tempo and balance (like a conductor of an orchestra) after the score has been stored in memory.

551. _____. "The digital computer as a musical
instrument." *Science* 142, 3592 (Nov. 1,
1963), 553.

A semi-technical description of MUSIC IV
and some of its applications is given.
Included are schematic diagrams of computer
instrument units, conversion of numbers to
sound pressure wave form, and an example of
a computer score. A distinction is drawn
between purely random and completely specified composition in computer music.

552. _____. A facility and program for generat-
ing and editing functions of time. Bell
Telephone Laboratories, Aug. 23, 1968. 6 pp.
Mimeo.

553. _____. "A graphical language for composing
and playing sounds and music." *Journal of
the Audio Engineering Society* 15, 1 (1967),
96. Abstract.

Speech sounds can be represented by graphical
functions of time-specifying formants. A
generalization of this graphical representation to other sounds and music is described.
Graphical functions of time are used to
represent pitch, loudness, and duration.
Computer sounds can be synthesized directly
from the functions drawn with a light pen
and oscilloscope.

554. _____. "Immediate sound generation." *Journal
of the Acoustical Society of America* 39, 6
(Jan. 1966), 1245. Abstract.

Also, presented to the 71st meeting of the
American Acoustical Society.

Description of procedures for immediate

synthesis of sound by means of a Packard-Bell 250 computer attached to an IBM 7094 computer.

555. _____. "Le studio de sons électroniques des années 70." *La Revue Musicale* 268-269 (1971), 125-137.

Also, as "The electronic sound studio of the 1970's." In *Music and Technology*. Paris: La Revue Musicale, 1971. 129-141.

The author projects the use of hybrid digital-analog sound systems in electronic music studios by the end of the 1970's. Following is a description of the GROOVE program and system, with diagrams of an 'instrument' specification and of the structure of a hybrid sound synthesizer.

556. _____; and Gerald Bennett. Real-time synthesizer control. Centre Georges Pompidou Rapports IRCAM No. 5, Paris, 1978.

The problem of controlling powerful digital synthesizers is discussed with some thoughts on the kinds of control that are possible and implications of each kind, in terms of the quality of control, the precision, and the speed.

557. _____; and Jie-Jih Chang. Score-drawing program. Audio Engineering Society preprint.

558. _____; and F.B. Denes. Computer models for speech and music appreciation. Bell Telephone Laboratories, Murray Hill, N.J., 1968.

Also, in *Proceedings of the AFIPS Conference* 33 (1968), 319-327.

Review of speech studies leading to programs for speech synthesis and algorithms for music composition, with special attention focused on the problems arising from long range dependencies in the sound sequence.

559. _____; and Newman Guttman. "Generation of music by a digital computer." in *Proceedings of the Third International Congress on Acoustics, Stuttgart, 1959.* Ed. L. Cremer. Amsterdam: Elsevier, 1961. I, 253-254.

560. _____; and Joan E. Miller. "Computer program for automatic composition and generation of music." *Journal of the Acoustical Society of America* 35, 11 (Nov. 1963), 1908. Abstract.

A new program (modification of previous work) with simplified notation and expanded capabilities is presented. Instrument definitions are made by listing elements of a basic diagram, with input specifications; the computer then generates the parameters. Repetition and transformation are now possible.

561. _____;_____. *Music 4 Programmer's Manual.* Murray Hill, N.J.: Bell Telephone Laboratories, 1965.

This handbook to the Music 4 program includes descriptions of routines and instructions for users. It was intended to be accompanied by a tape of the card images of the program and a memorandum on the BEFAP compiler. There is also an outline for the adaptation of Music 4 to any IBM 7090-7094 installation.

562. _____; _____. "Pitch quantizing for computer music." *Journal of the Acoustical Society of America* 38, 11 (Nov. 1965), 913. Abstract.

A program is described that 'quantizes' the frequencies of a series of computer-generated notes, i.e. combined requirements of vertical and horizontal intervals may be constructed. The program has been used to generalize various harmonizations while specifying melodies within certain intervals, diatonic scales, or twelve-tone scales.

563. _____; _____; F.R. Moore; John R. Pierce; and Jean-Claude Risset. *The Technology of Computer Music.* Boston: MIT Press, 1969. 188 pp.

This book is intended as a textbook of computer-generated music and gives full details on the MUSIC V program developed by the author at Bell Telephone Laboratories. The first section deals with such topics as sampling and quantizing, with mathematical analyses, foldover error, sample and hold analysis, bounding sample errors, D/A and A/D converters, smoothing filter design, data storage and retrieval for sound, and fundamental programming problems. Sets of problems to be solved by the student are included, as well as annotated references and two appendices on psychoacoustics and mathematics relevant to the text. The complete manual for the MUSIC V program, indexed for references, constitutes the final section of the book.

564. _____; _____; and John R. Pierce.
"Computer study of trumpet tones." *Journal of the Audio Engineering Society* 38, 5 (1965), 912-913. Abstract.

565. _____; _____; _____; and James Tenney. "Computer study of violin tones." *Journal of the Acoustical Society of America* 38, 11 (1965), 912-913. Abstract.

Complete report presented as *Bell Telephone Laboratories Internal Report.* Murray Hill, N.J., 1966.

Violin tones as well as trumpet tones in the above study were digitized and analyzed by computer. Amplitude of each harmonic was plotted and features of the spectrum noted. A theory involving the nature of excitation by the bow was developed and tones were resynthesized as a check on the theory.

566. _____; and F.R. Moore. "GROOVE-- a computer program for real time music and sound synthesis." *Journal of the Acoustical Society of America* 47, 1: part 1 (Jan.1970), 132. Abstract.

Also, presented at the 78th convention of the American Acoustical Society, San Diego, Cal., Nov. 4-7, 1969.

567. _____; _____. "GROOVE, a program for real-time control of a sound synthesizer by a computer." *Proceedings of the American Society of University Composers* 4 (1971), 27-31.

Above articles describe a system which allows a performer to modify programmed instruction stored by a small computer (the DDP-224) in real time, with the new combination of instructions being stored in memory. These instructions are transformed to control voltages and 'played back' on the synthesizer.

568. _____ ; _____ . "GROOVE-- a program to compare store and edit functions of time." *Communications of the Association for Computing Machinery* 13, 12 (Dec. 1970), 715-721.

Technical description of the same program presented in above articles. The program was conceived as a general-purpose program for digital control of any analog device.

569. _____ ; _____ ; and Jean-Claude Risset. "Computers and future music." *Science* 183, 4122 (Jan. 25, 1974), 263-268.

Reprinted in *Numus West* [Mercer Island, Washington] 6 (1974), 40-47.

Also, as *Computers and Future Music*. Murray Hill, N.J.: Acoustical and Behavioral Research Center, 1974.

Brief descriptions are given of MUSIC V (program for sound generation), GROOVE (program for hybrid digital control of analog equipment), and a catalogue of digital sounds and sound-studies made by Risset.

570. _____; John R. Pierce; and N. Guttman. "Musical sounds from digital computers." *Gravesäner Blatter* 6, 23-24 (1962), 119-125.

Reprinted as "The sound of music from digital computers." *Institute of Electronic and Electrical Engineers Student Journal* 1, 4 (Sept. 1963), 25.

An introduction to computer-generated sound. Explanations are given for the principle of sampling, computer instruments, the computer score, and psychoacoustic matters.

571. _____; _____; and Jean-Claude Risset. "Further experiments on the use of the computer in connection with music." *Gravesaner Blätter* 27-28 (Nov. 1965), 92-97.

A semi-technical description of applications of MUSIC IV is given. Tenney's study of the influence of the attack envelope on timbre is mentioned. Diagrams and bibliography included.

572. _____; and L. Rosler. "Graphical language for the scores of computer-generated sounds." *Perspectives of New Music* 6, 2 (1968), 92-118.

Also, in *Music by Computers,* ed. by Heinz von Foerster and J.W. Beauchamp. New York: Wiley and Sons, 1969. 71-83.

Abstract appears in *Journal of the Audio Engineering Society of America* 40, 5 (Nov. 1966), 1252.

A method for drawing a score as a graphical
function of time by using a light pen on a
cathode ray tube (as a replacement for
punched data cards) is described in detail.
This procedure allows for sound sequences
to be developed by trial and error and then
saved on punched cards or microfilm. The
program also provides the possibility of
combining graphical functions by addition
or multiplication, resulting in an 'aver-
aging' process between two melodic or rhythmic lines, or a gradual transition from one
line to another. Recorded examples are
provided.

573. _____. See Chang and Mathews.

574. _____. See Lawson and Mathews.

575. _____. See Risset and Mathews.

576. _____. See Strasser and Mathews.

577. Matthews, Justus Frederick. *HDORYUT (composed
with Musical Instruction Composition
Oriented Language MUSICOL)*. Diss., State
University of New York at Buffalo, 1973.

578. McCauley, C.S. *Computers and Creativity*.
New York: Praeger, 1974. 160 pp.

Intent of this book is to draw attention
to the ways in which the computer has
begun to be a tool for the artist and
musician. Numerous errors in minor details.

579. McGill, James F. Music synthesis by optimal
filtering. Paper presented at the First
International Conference on Computer
Music, Massachussetts Institute of Technology, Oct. 29-31, 1976.

The optimal filter, which has been used in the analysis and resynthesis of speech, is used here for the synthesis of musical instrument sounds. The filter-driving function is neither a string of impulses nor a white noise source, but the true error function of the optimal filter.

580. Melby, Carol. *Computer Music Compositions of the United States, 1976*. Prepared for the First International Conference on Computer Music, Massachussetts Institute of Technology, Oct. 28-31, 1976. Urbana, Ill.: Carol Melby, 1976. Distributed by Theodore Front Musical Literature, Beverly Hills, Cal.

Compilation of original works, both published and unpublished, which are realized or composed by means of computers. The criterion for inclusion in this listing was that the composer be a United States citizen, working in the U.S., or currently living in the U.S. Ninety-one composers who responded to questionnaires are represented. The emphasis is on work done at large installations at universities.

581. Melby, John, moderator. "Compositional approaches to computer music." (Panel discussion with David Cohen, Charles Dodge, Hubert S. Howe, Donald MacInnis and Barry Vercoe.) *Proceedings of the American Society of University Composers* 1 (1972-73), 22-30.

David Cohen suggests the use of computer-generated realizations of compositions as a rehearsal aid; Hubert Howe discusses the orchestration and compositional process of his computer-generated work *Freeze*.

582. _____. Compositional approaches to the combination of live performers with computer-produced tape. Paper presented at the First International Conference on Computer Music, Massachussetts Institute of Technology, Oct. 28-31, 1976.

Because digital synthesis makes it possible to accomplish musical/technical feats heretofore impossible, the author sees special problems in combining such tapes with live performance and discusses them here.

583. _____. A method of controlling local and large scale relationships in twelve-tone and other serial compositions. Diss., Princeton University, 1972. *Dissertation Abstracts* 34, 2 (Aug. 1973), 811A.

584. _____. "Some recent developments in computer-synthesized music." *Proceedings of the American Society of University Composers* 5 (1970), 111-121.

A brief explanation of digital sound synthesis is given, mentioning MUSIC 4B, MUSIC 4BF, Music 360, voice synthesis programs by Godfrey Winham, and a program for real-time synthesis being developed at Oberlin.

585. _____. See Beauchamp and Melby.

586. Ménard, Phillippe. "Présentation du programme AUTOMUSE." *Artinfo-Musinfo* 15 (1973), 19-37.

587. Menchinelli, S. A microcomputer approach to the polyphonic music synthesizer. Paper presented to the 56th convention of the Audio Engineering Society, Paris, March 1-4, 1977. Preprint No. 1211.

A polyphonic synthesizer system, which utilizes the SC/MP 8-bit microprocessor interfaced to ten digitally controlled monophonic synthesizers, is described. A keyboard is provided as the input controller.

588. Metzge, G.; and J. Bauknight. Magical Music Maker: a four-part music-making program for the Illiac II. Urbana: University of Illinois Digital Computer Laboratory File No. 609, July 12, 1964. Mimeo.

589. Meyers, Roger. See Chadabe and Meyers.

590. Mezer, Leslie. See Buxton, Reeves, Baecker, and Mezer.

591. Miller, J.E. See Mathews and Miller.

592. _____. See Mathews, Miller, Pierce, and Tenney.

593. _____. See Mathews, Miller, Moore, Pierce, and Risset.

594. Mintner, Thomas. "Art and technology at the University of Iowa (Iowa City)." *Numus West* [Mercer Island, Washington] 2, 1 (Winter 1975), 29-32.

Activities at the University of Iowa are described. The author also describes his own on-going design and construction of a modular system featuring analog control

devices with 'local' module memories, a
microprocessor, and digital tape unit to
be used both for visual control of a laser
system and for electronic sound-processing
and control.

595. Mohring, Phillipp. "Können technische, insbesondere
Computer-Erzeugnisse Werke der Literatur,
Musik, und Malerei sein?" *A. für Urheber-,
Film-, Funk-, und Theaterrecht* 50, 100
(1967), 835-843.

The author's conclusion is that computer-
produced music is copyrightable only if
the work has been completely pre-determined
by the programmer.

596. Moles, Abraham Andre. "Art and cybernetics in
the supermarket." In *Cybernetics, the Arts,
and Ideas,* ed. Jasia Reichardt. Greenwich,
Connecticut: New York Graphic Society, Ltd.,
1971. 61-71.

Discussion of aesthetic attitudes that bring
an artist or musician to consider a machine
as a generator of new ideas or of all possibilities in nature; or as a means of carrying
an idea to its logical or extreme conclusion;
or as a means of systematically making all
possible permutations of a set of elements
(visual or acoustic); or a simulation of art
processes; or a visual sum of a series of
images in time, i.e. integration of forms.

597. _____. *Art et ordinateur*. Paris: Casterman,
1971. 190-222.

598. _____. "Le Centre de Musique expérimentale
H. Scherchen à Gravesano." *Revue du Son*
37 (May 1956), 113.

599. _____. "Instrumentation électronique et
musiques expérimentales." *La Revue Musicale*
244 (1959), 40–49.

The concept of a 'sonorous object' is
described as applicable to musique concrète
and sound structures generated electronically.
A simple scheme for a machine to compose
music (to produce 'sonorous objects') is
presented and the work of Mathews and
Guttman is cited. The author makes several
points concerning the use of technology by
composers.

600. _____. "Machines à musiques." *La Revue
Musicale* 236 (1957), 115–127.

Developments in the synthesis of speech at
this time are noted and sound synthesis
instruments (Melochord, Mixtur-Trautonium,
Vocoder, and others) are described. A
distinction is made between semantic
information and aesthetic information con-
veyed by synthesized sounds.

601. _____. *Machines à musique: du Phonogène
au Vocoder.* Numero spécial sur les
musiques expérimentales. Paris: Richard
Masse, 1957.

602. _____. "La musique algorithmique, première
musique calculée." *Revue de Son* 93, 1
(1961), n.p.

603. _____. *Les Musiques expérimentales.* Paris:
Editions du Cercle d'Art Contemporaine,
1960. 166 pp.

Discussion of electronic music and the
recent use of computers, with particular
emphasis on the applicability of informa-

tion theory to these musics. A bibliography, list of works presented on the radio, and a short discography are included.

604. _____. "The new relationship between music and mathematics." *Gravesaner Blätter* 23/24 (1962), 98-108.

Use of computers in creative activity is seen as a new stage in music history, representing a step beyond mechanical reproduction. This changes the function of art in society and the role of the composer. The composer supplies ideas which engender a host of possible 'realizations.' This leads to an experimental attitude. The machine may be used also to discover how works of art are produced-- a problem of aesthetics, not an artistic problem.

605. _____. "Perspectives de l'instrumentation électronique." *Revue Belge de Musicologie* 13 (1959), 11-25.

Apologia for musique concrète and the idea of the 'sonorous object' is given. Various instruments for producing 'objets sonores' include the Vocoder. The author uses information theory applied to music as his guiding light.

606. _____. "The prospects of electronic instrumentation." *Gravesaner Blätter* 15/16 (1960), 21-44.

Also presented at a conference, Journées de Musique Experimentale de Bruxelles, Oct. 1958.

Experimental music, the importance of the advent of tape recording to the nature of music today, and synthetic sound generation are discussed. Electrical composition by machines as a model of a brain's creative activity is speculated upon.

607. _____. *Théorie de l'information et perception esthétique.* Paris: Flammarion, 1958.

Also, as *Information Theory and Esthetic Perception.* Trans. Joel E. Cohen. Urbana, Ill.: University of Illinois Press, 1966.

Physical information theory is outlined and then applied to artistic structures, semantic information, and aesthetic information. This book provides a theoretical basis for the experiments of Hiller, Mathews, Barbaud, Fucks, and others. The author makes a critique of music theory and proposes his concept of the 'sonorous object' as appropriate to a theory for electronic music and musique concrète.

608. Moog, Robert A. Digital-controlled electronic music modules. Paper presented to the 37th convention of the Audio Engineering Society, New York, Oct. 13-16, 1969.

609. _____. "Introduction to programmed control." *Electronic Music Review* 1 (Jan. 1967), 23-29, 32.

Discussion of techniques for the use of the sequencer, punched paper tape reader, and a hybrid digital/analog sound generating system, as well as a large digital computer with a D/A converter.

610. _____. "An objective look at electronic music equipment." *Proceedings of the American Society of University Composers* 4 (1971), 32-35.

Discusses problem of using small computers for programming analog oscillators, which tend to drift 1 or 2% over several days, and programs which try to compensate for this. The author also cites several advantages of the computer-controlled studio.

611. Moore, B. Hybrid synthesizers. Paper presented to the 53rd convention of the Audio Engineering Society, Zurich, March 2-5, 1976.

Also, presented to the 54th convention of the AES, Los Angeles, May 4-7, 1976. Preprint No. 1129.

A system is described which employs a microprocessor, a simple program, D/A interface, and voltage-controllable hardware. A portable prototype system was demonstrated.

612. Moore, F. Richard. GROOVE-- a program for composing and editing functions of time in real-time. Bell Telephone Laboratories Report, Murray Hill, N.J., March 1969.

613. _____. "An introduction to the mathematics of digital signal processing. Part I: algebra, trigonometry, and the most beautiful formula in mathematics." *Computer Music Journal* 2, 1 (July 1978), 38-47.

The basic mathematical ideas needed to approach the topic of data processing are presented here for musicians with an interest in musical data processing. Fourier's theorem is given and explained.

614. _____. "An introduction to the mathematics
of digital signal processing. Part II:
sampling, transforms, and digital filtering." *Computer Music Journal* 2, 2
(Sept. 1978), 38-60.

Application of basic concepts outlined in
Part I, above. Sampling and quantization,
digital signals, spectra, the discrete
Fourier transform, convolution, the
Z-transform, and digital filtering are
all discussed. A list of references on
several relevant topics is included.

615. _____. "Musica ed elaboratori eletronici."
Encyclopedia della scienza e della tecnica
(1971), 490-498.

616. _____. "Table look-up noise for sinusoidal
digital oscillators." *Computer Music
Journal* 1, 2 (April 1977), 26-29.

The most economical method of generating
sinusoids digitally seems to be the
table look-up method. Charts for signal-to-
error noise ratios corresponding to the
various ways of implementing the method are
included and discussed.

617. _____. See Mathews and Moore.

618. _____. See Mathews, Moore, and Risset.

619. _____. See Mathews, Miller, Moore, Pierce,
and Risset.

620. Moore, Robert. "New music at Oberlin in the 70's."
Numus West [Mercer Island, Washington]
1, 5 (1974), 53-55.

Description of activities at Oberlin
Conservatory, including music/technology
program, digital installation featuring
MUSIC IV and MUSIC V programs by M. Mathews,
and a hybrid system being designed by
Sergio Franco.

621. Moorer, James A. "How does a computer make music?"
Computer Music Journal 2, 1 (July 1978),
32-37.

Basic explanation of digital sound generation. An example of an 'instrument definition' and 'note list' in MUS10 (a music
compiler from Stanford University) is
given. Charts and references are included.

622. _____. "Music and computer composition."
*Communications of the Association for
Computing Machinery* 15, 2 (Feb. 1972),
104-113.

Simulated examples of Western popular music
have been created by computer and are described here. Problems with this kind of
program are discussed. The *Illiac Suite*
of Hiller and Isaacson is also discussed.

623. _____. On the loudness of complex time-variant tones. Stanford University Department
of Music Technical Report, STAN-M-4,
Stanford, California, 1975.

Reprint of part of a proposal to the
National Science Foundation division of
psychobiology. The perception of loudness
in complex time-variant tones is to be
studied, with some possible revision of
current theories of loudness. Tones are
digitally synthesized for the gathering of
physical data and perceived results.

624. _____. On the segmentation and analysis of continuous musical sound by digital computer. Diss., Stanford University, 1975. Distributed as Department of Music Technical Report STAN-M-3.

A two-voice polyphonic composition was digitized and stored in computer memory. A procedure was devised for analyzing the digitized waveform and automatically producing a written manuscript in standard musical notation, using Leland Smith's MSS program for the manuscripting.

625. _____. "The optimum comb method of pitch period analysis of continuous digitized speech." *IEEE Transactions on Acoustics, Speech and Signal Processing* ASSP-22 (Oct. 1974), 330-338.

A new method of tracking the fundamental frequency of voiced speech is described.

626. _____. "Reply by Moorer." *Communications of the Association for Computing Machinery* 15 (1972), 1001. See also, Smoliar (#940).

627. _____. "Signal processing aspects of computer music: a survey." *Proceedings of the Institute of Electronic and Electrical Engineers* 65, 8 (Aug. 1977), 1108-1137.

Reprinted in *Computer Music Journal* 1, 1 (1977), 4-37.

A survey is made of the use of analysis of natural sounds, the use of speech and vocoder techniques, methods of artificial reverberation, the use of discrete summation formulae for highly efficient synthesis and the concept of the all-digital recording studio in the production and processing of musical sounds. The role of special purpose hardware in digital music synthesis is discussed, illustrated by two unique digital music synthesizers (one designed by F.R. Moore, the other by Peter Samson). Many diagrams and a list of references are included.

628. _____. " The synthesis of complex audio spectra by means of discrete summation formulas." *Journal of the Audio Engineering Society* 24, 9 (Nov. 1976), 717-727.

Also, as Stanford University Department of Music Technical Report STAN-M-5 (Dec. 1975).

A new family of synthesis techniques which provide a means of controlling the spectra of audio signals has been discovered and is described here in full. It has the advantages of control and flexibility of J. Chowning's frequency modulation technique. In addition, it allows a signal to be limited to an exact number of partials, and 'one-sided' spectra can be conveniently synthesized. Diagrams and MUSIC V-type illustrations are provided.

629. _____. The use of the linear prediction of speech in computer music application. Centre Georges Pompidou Rapports IRCAM No. 6, Paris, 1978.

Also, presented to the 59th convention of the Audio Engineering Society, Hamburg, Feb. 28 - March 3, 1978. Preprint No. 1320.

It is possible to design a digital filter
which approximates the spectrum of a time-
variant waveform at certain intervals of
time using linear prediction algorithms.
This type of filter has been found useful
in speech synthesis and analysis. In the
applications discussed here, it is possible
to change pitch of pre-recorded materials
without altering the timing, or vice versa,
with the use of these algorithms, and to
blend sounds of instruments and voices in
a unique way.

630. _____. "The use of the phase vocoder in
computer music applications." *Journal
of the Audio Engineering Society* 26, 1/2
(Jan./Feb. 1978), 42-45.

Also, presented to the 55th convention of
the Audio Engineering Society, New York,
Oct. 29, 1976. Preprint No. 1146.

Also, presented at the First International
Conference on Computer Music, Massachussetts
Institute of Technology, Oct. 28-31, 1976.

A theoretical explanation of the phase
vocoder as an analysis-synthesis system
is first given. The linear predictor is
a device used to hold the time-variant
discrete Fourier spectrum constant, and
therefore preserving the vowel quality,
as the pitch is changed. This is explained
in detail.

631. _____. See Chowning, Grey, Moorer, and Rush.

632. _____. See Grey and Moorer.

633. _____. See Rush and Moorer.

634. _____. See Rush, Moorer, and Loy.

635. _____; and John Grey. "Lexicon of analyzed tones-- part 1: a violin tone." *Computer Music Journal* 1, 2 (April 1977), 39-45.

Numerous analysis and plotting programs are presented here, with editorial notes by John Snell, the editor of the journal. These were produced at the Center for Computer Research in Music and Acoustics at Stanford University as part of dissertation work by the authors.

636. _____; _____. "Lexicon of analyzed tones-- part 2: clarinet and oboe tones." *Computer Music Journal* 1, 3 (June 1977), 12-29.

Accompanying text is a tutorial on timbre, analysis and synthesis of complex tones, and characteristics of the instruments being studied. Editorial notes by J. Strawn.

637. _____; _____. "Lexicon of analyzed tones-- part 3: the trumpet." *Computer Music Journal* 2, 2 (Sept. 1978), 23-31.

Analysis and plotting diagrams which describe the timbral characteristics of the trumpet are given here. Tables of line segment approximation data for oboe and clarinet tones are also included. Editorial notes by J. Strawn.

638. Morrill, Dexter. "Trumpet algorithms for computer composition." *Computer Music Journal* 1, 1 (1977), 25-30.

Previous acoustic studies of trumpet tones are discussed and a detailed description is given of a frequency modulation instrument with input data for a very realistic synthesized trumpet tone. Diagrams and coded instruction are included. The design and data are to be used as the basis for further timbral variations.

639. "Musique et machines." *Faire* [Bourges: Editions GMEB] 2/3 (1975), 183-206.

Panel discussion between Coriun Aharonian, Jon Appleton, Pierre Boeswillwald, William Buxton, W. Kotonski, Leo Kupper, and Phillipe Menard.

640. Nelson, Gary. "COMPOSE: a program for musical composition." *Computational Musicology Newsletter* 1, 1 (Oct. 1973), 11.

Also, presented at the International Conference on Computers in the Humanities, Minneapolis, Minn., July 21, 1973.

Figures, examples, and tables are presented for a program which is to generate a piece from rules, parameters, and general sound contours indicated by the composer. As an example of the output, an excerpt of a duet for flute and bassoon is given.

641. _____. "MPL: a program library for musical data processing." *Creative Computing* (March/April 1977), 76-81.

Description of a sound synthesis program
at Oberlin Conservatory of Music. The
program is written in APL and run on a
Xerox (now Honeywell) SIGMA 9 computer.
Based conceptually on Chowning's frequency
modulation technique, it is employed for
composition, demonstrations of exotic scales,
and aural skills tests. Programming is
provided for printed output in standard
musical notation.

642. Neufeld, Ludvik. "Spracovanie piesňových nápevov
na samočinných počítačoch v Maďarsku."
Lidová píseň a samočinný počítač I, ed.
Dušan Holý and Oldřich Sirovátka [Brno:
Klub uživatelů MSP, 1972] 203-206.

643. Neumann, P. G. See Brooks, Neumann, and Wright.

644. _____; and H. Schappert. "Komponieren mit
elektronishen Rechenautomaten." *Nachrichten-
technische Zeitschrift* 12 (1959), 403-407.

Abstract in *Annales des Telecommunications*
14 (1959), 1364.

The process of composition itself is studied
and experimental work in simulating compositional processes is described briefly.

645. Nosselt, Volker. The problem of 'klingen' in the
context of acoustical theories. Paper
presented at the 2nd Central Europe section
convention of the Audio Engineering Society,
Munich, March 14-16, 1972.

The musical sensation of 'klingen' (sounding)
is discussed as it relates to electroacoust-
ical sonorisation and music reproduction
and to acoustical theories.

Nosselt, continued

646. _____. "Die programmierte elektroakustische
     Musikrealisation mittels elektronischer
     Digital-Datenverarbeitungsanlage. Die
     Programmierung-- ein musikalisches
     Steuerungsproblem." *IPEM-Yearbook*
     [Seminar of Musicology, Ghent State
     University, Netherlands] 2 (1967).

     Three topics are discussed: 1) problems
     of programming sound wave structures of
     musical systems, 2) pre-determining the
     auditory results, and 3) the effect of
     room acoustics on the musical realization.

647. O'Beirne, T.H. "Computer programs which play
     music with microtones." *Computer Journal*
     13 (1970), 344-349.

     A program called ORPHEUS for the SOLIDAC
     computer (made in the U.K. by Barr and
     Stroud, Ltd.) accepts transcribed scores
     as input which can be modified and played
     back, with microtonal tunings being a
     possibility. Sound is obtained by directly
     amplifying pulse waves produced by an
     internal circuit in the computing equipment,
     whose frequency is determined by the
     programming. The author has produced 12-,
     19-, 31-, and 53-tone equal-tempered
     scales using this method.

648. _____. "Music from paper tape." In
     Cybernetic Serendipity, ed. Jasia Reichardt.
     New York: Praeger, 1969. 29-30.

     Reprinted from the *Bulletin of the Institute
     of Mathematics and its Applications* 6 (1970),
     68-69.

154

The author describes his system of producing tones from an internal circuit in
a high-speed computer. The circuit itself
is made to oscillate at various frequencies
by programming loops using punched paper input.

649. _____. "Music, numbers, and computers."
    *Bulletin of the Institute of Mathematics
    and its Applications* 3, 57-66.

650. Oehlschlagel, Reinhard. "Neue Musik von A-Z."
    Opern Welt (July 1970), 43.

    Chronological overview of 'computer music.'
    Mention is made of the work of Hiller and
    Isaacson, Ferentzy, Robert Baker, Xenakis,
    Tenney, Koenig, and Barbaud. Chance and
    random procedures as a philosophical basis
    for music produced by these methods is
    discussed in brief.

651. Olive, Joseph. The use of the digital computer
    in the generation of music. Paper presented
    at the Midwest Acoustics Conference, Evanston,
    Illinois, April 5, 1975.

    New developments in digital sound synthesis
    at Bell Laboratories are discussed. Topics
    include digital synthesis of complex timbres,
    real-time music generation projects in-
    volving hybrid systems, and applications
    of speech sounds in music.

652. Olson, Harry F. "Electronic music synthesis for
    recordings." *Institute of Electronic and
    Electrical Engineering Spectrum* 8, 4
    (April 1971), 18-30.

    The basic procedure of digital synthesis

is outlined, after Max Mathews' programs. Diagrams included.

653. _____; and Herbert Belar. "Aid to music composition employing a random probability system." *Journal of the Acoustical Society of America* 33 (1961), 1163-1170.

The authors describe their 'composing machine,' which uses statistical analysis of Stephen Foster's tunes for input information to produce similar tunes. Included are schematic diagrams of the various generators, read-out systems and master control, probability matrix and decode system, and sound synthesizer, plus examples of the musical output.

654. Oppenheim, David. "Microcomputer to synthesizer interface for a low cost system." *Computer Music Journal* 2,1 (July 1978), 6-11.

A general-purpose microcomputer system is discussed here. A Zilog Z-80 microprocessor with a floppy disk memory and terminal of some sort is recommended, with various options for hardware (commercial synthe-- sizers, user-built modules, or digital circuits) and software. The necessities for timing and an analog interface are discussed and a minimum-hardware circuit for this purpose is presented.

655. "Optical electronics provides computer music." *Electro-Optical Systems Design* 10, 12 (Dec. 1978), 6-7.

A polyphonic keyboard interface and control system that uses opto-electronic components, being developed by Professors Dworak and Parker at Carnegie-Mellon University, is described here. This project was presented at the First International Computer Music Conference at Cambridge, Mass., and also at the Second International Conference on Computer Music at San Diego, Cal.

656. O'Haver, T.C. "Audio processing with a micro-processor." *Byte* 3, 6 (June 1978), 166-173.

Discussion of the use of a microprocessor (1K-5K bytes of programmable memory) and D/A and A/D converters. This set-up, plus software, may be used for waveform modification (controlled distortion), time delay, phase shift, and reverberation effects. A short glossary of terms is provided.

657. _____. "More music for the 6502." *Byte* 3, 6 (June 1978), 140-141.

Simple tone sequences in just intonation are generated; governing controls are based on arithmetic or Boolean relations and a simple waveform table is used. Hardware is MOS Technology 6502 based computer with 1K bytes of programmable memory and an 8-bit D/A converter.

658. Oram, Daphne. "Oramics." *Musical Events* 23, 11 (Nov. 1968), 6-7.

659. Otis, Alton B. An analog input/output system for the Illiac II. University of Illinois Experimental Music Studio Technical Report No. 17, Urbana, Sept. 1967. 72 pp.

660. _____. Artificial reverberation. University of Illinois Experimental Music Studio Technical Report No. 14, Urbana, Sept. 1968. 16-37.

661. _____. "Low-pass digital filtration." In Four Sound Processing Programs for the Illiac II Computer and D/A Converter, ed. James W. Beauchamp. University of Illinois Experimental Music Studio Technical Report No. 14, Urbana, Sept. 1968, 1-15.

662. _____. "Time rate changing." In Four Sound Processing Programs for the Illiac II Computer and D/A Converter, ed. James W. Beauchamp. University of Illinois Experimental Music Studio Technical Report No. 14, Urbana, Sept. 1968, 38-49.

663. _____. See Beauchamp, Otis, Grossman, Cuomo.

664. Otsuki, S. "An attempt at machine composition by machine experience." *Information Processing in Japan* 4 (1964), n.p. In Jap. (Available at the IBM research library, Yorktown, N.Y.)

665. Padberg, Mother Harriet Ann R.S.C.J. Computer-composed canon and free fugue. Diss., St. Louis University, 1964. *Dissertation Abstracts* 26, 4 (1965), 2240.

   Description of composition based on a microtonal scale taken from the higher harmonics of the harmonic series, realized by digital sound synthesis. The canon was composed with a FORTRAN program and IBM 1620 and 7094 computers. Group theory also played a part in the composition of this work.

666. Pala, Karel. "Možnosti popisu sémantiky lidové písně." *Lidová píseň a samočinný počítač I*, ed. Dušan Holý and Oldřich Sirovátka. Brno: Klub uživatelů MSP, 1972. 63-77.

667. "Papers from the 1977 International Computer Music Conference." *Computer Music Journal* 2, 3 (Dec. 1978), 43.

Papers presented at this conference were not published. Xerox copies of manuscripts are offered here.

668. Papworth, D.G. "Computers and change-ringing." *Computer Journal* 3 (1960–61), 47–50.

A program for systematically producing the various combinations of ringing six bells, according to certain rules, is presented. These rules, as applied to 'plain bob major,' are described.

669. Pask, Gordon. "A comment, a case history, and a plan." In *Cybernetics, the Arts, and Ideas,* ed. Jasia Reichardt. Greenwich, Conn.: New York Graphic Society, 1971. 76–99.

A system for relating visual images and sound, 'Musicolor,' is described in its several versions. The machine included a 'learning capability' which allowed visual and audio relationships to be modified as the performance goes on. Moving light and sound mobiles were also added. These were programmed to operate according to human-like behavioral patterns. The system was used by Jane Parry as an aid to composition and performance.

670. Patrick, P.H. "Composer, computer, and audience." *Composer* 35 (Spring 1970), 1–3.

671. Pedersen, Birte Litrup; and Henrik Svane. Dansk elektronisk musik. Thesis, University of Aarhus, 1975.

672. Pennycook, Bruce. "Review." *Computer Music Journal* 2, 4 (late Dec. 1978), 6-9.

Review of W. Zimmerman's *Desert Plants* (Vancouver: W. Zimmerman and ARC Publications, 1978). See Zimmerman.

673. People's Computer Company. *Computer Music Journal*. Box E, Menlo Park, Calif. Now published by MIT Press, Cambridge, Mass.

A journal which includes articles on computer-aided analysis; editing and printing of sheet music; digital synthesis; microcomputer control of digital or analog synthesizers; new keyboards and other controllers; digital filtering; tunings applicable to computer music systems; D/A and A/D converters; analysis of acoustic instrument tones; psychoacoustics; and other relevant topics. Founding editor was John Snell. Current (1980) editor is Curtis Roads. John Strawn is editorial assistant.

674. _____. *Doctor Dobb's Journal (of Computer Calisthenics and Orthodontia)*. Box E, Menlo Park, Calif.

A publication for computer hobbyists. It includes evaluations of new products, much information on software for microcomputers and occasional articles dealing more directly with applications to audio and to music.

675. Perrot, Michel. "Entretien avec Iannis Xenakis." *La Revue Musicale* 265-266 (1969), 61-76.

Interview with Xenakis.

160

676. Petersen, Tracy Lind. Analysis-synthesis as a tool for creating new families of sound. Paper presented at the 54th convention of the Audio Engineering Society, Los Angeles, May 4-7, 1976. Preprint No. 1104.

Established techniques for analysis-synthesis of speech may be used to produce unusual sounds for musical purposes. These include musical instruments articulating human speech and musical signals modulated by the time-varying spectral characteristics of other musical signals.

677. _____. Composing with cross-synthesis. Paper presented at the First International Conference on Computer Music, Massachussetts Institute of Technology, Oct. 28-31, 1976.

The composer discusses his composition *Everything and Nothing,* which includes computer-synthesized voices and motivic timbral elements derived from the composer's technique of 'cross-synthesis' of different instruments.

678. _____. Dynamic sound processing. In Proceedings of the 1976 ACM Computer Science Conference, Anaheim, California, Feb. 10-12, 1976.

679. _____. "Vocal tract modulation of instrumental sounds by digital filtering." In *Software Synthesis Techniques,* Proceedings of the Second Annual Music Computation Conference, Nov. 7-9, 1975, part 1. Urbana: University of Illinois, 1975. 33-41.

Description of the author's own technique
of synthesizing musical sounds that seem
to be articulated by speech. A time-varying
digital filter, based on analysis of speech
input, is formulated by a linear-prediction
type vocoder. Synthetic speech is then
produced by applying the filter parameters
to a pulse train or to white noise, or in
this application, to a musical source.

680. Peutz, V.M.A. The variable acoustics of the
Espace de Projection of IRCAM (Paris).
Paper presented to the 59th convention
of the Audio Engineering Society, Hamburg,
Feb. 28–March 3, 1978. Preprint No. 1310.

A hall with variable form, volume, and
acoustics at the Institut de Recherche
et Coordination Acoustique/ Musique (IRCAM)
is described. Acoustic considerations for
spatially variable rooms are outlined and
a few remarks on the general aims of the
Institut are also included.

681. Philippot, Michel P. "La certitude et la for."
La Revue Musicale 257 (1963), 13–22.

Discussion of Xenakis as either a
Pythagorean or one who seeks to model
art upon nature.

682. _____. "La musique et les machines."
*Situation de la Recherche, Cahiers d'Etudes
de Radio-Television* 27–28 (1960), 274–292.

Historical account of developments in the
use of computers, mathematical procedures,
and chance or random processes in music.

683. _____. "Reflections of a composition teacher and radio man." *World Music* 15, 1 (1973), 21-35.

The mission of the O.R.T.F. in Paris and the future of music are discussed.

684. _____. "Vingt ans de musique." *Revue d'Esthetique* 4 (1967), 352-375.

A survey of the principle ideological currents that have influenced contemporary music since 1945, including the impact of the computer and mathematical methods applied to music.

685. Pierce, John R. "Attaining consonance in arbitrary scales." *Journal of the Acoustical Society of America* 40, 1 (July 1966), 249.

A digital computer was used to synthesize a scale of tones with fundamentals one-eighth octave apart; each tone had non-harmonic partials separated by one-fourth octave or multiples thereof. Rules of consonance and dissonance were then formulated. This project was part of on-going research at Bell Telephone Laboratories.

686. _____. "A chance for art." In *Cybernetics, Arts and Ideas,* ed. Jasia Reichardt. Greenwich, Ct.: New York Graphic Society, 1971. 46-56.

Remarks on the theory of communications, cybernetics, probability theory, and their applications to language, visual arts, and music.

687. _____. "Computers and music." *New Scientist* 25 (Feb. 18, 1965), 423–424.

Reprinted in *Cybernetic Serendipity*, ed. Jasia Reichardt. New York: Praeger, 1969; London: McKay, 1968. 18–19.

A history of the use of the computer as a source of sound.

688. _____. "The computer as a musical instrument." (letter to the editor). *Journal of the Audio Engineering Society* 8, 2 (April 1960), 139–140.

Report on work by Mathews and Guttman at Bell Telephone Laboratories, Murray Hill, N.J., with first simple musical experiments listed. The work of Hiller and Isaacson is also mentioned.

689. _____. "Portrait of the machine as a young artist." *Playboy* 12, 6 (June 1965), 124+.

690. _____. *Symbols, Signals, and Noise.* New York: Harper, 1961. 305 pp.

Chapter 8 on information theory and art deals directly with questions of information processing capacity of human beings and information in musical compositions and other questions of relevance to composers using computers. The general topic of communications theory is tangential to computer-aided musical composition.

691. _____; and Max V. Mathews. "Control of
consonance and dissonance with non-harmonic
overtones." In *Music by Computers,* ed.
Heinz von Foerster and James W. Beauchamp.
New York: Wiley and Sons, 1969. 129-132.

Experimentation with non-harmonic overtones
in various spacings is described. The "Eight
Tone Canon" by J.R. Pierce was an outcome
of this research and is included in the
recording accompanying this book.

692. _____. See Mathews, Miller, Pierce, and
Tenney.

693. _____. See Mathews and Pierce.

694. _____. See Mathews, Pierce, and Guttman.

695. _____. See Mathews, Pierce, Miller, Moore,
and Risset.

696. _____. See Mathews, Pierce, and Risset.

697. Pignon, Paul. See Buxton and Pignon.

698. Pinkerton, R.C. "Information theory and melody."
Scientific American 194, 76 (1956), 77.

699. Pinzarrone, Joseph. "Interactive woman-machine
improvisation or live computer-music performed by dance." *Creative Computing* 3,
2 (1977), 66.

Also presented at the First International
Conference on Computer Music, Massachussetts
Institute of Technology, Oct. 28-31, 1976.

A report is given here on a project that
aims to relate movement and sound, realized

165

through an original hybrid system. Hardware includes a PDP11/10 computer and an analog synthesizer, with an interface. Connected to the data bus is a 64-bit gravity-sensor body costume designed for real-time performance. A chronicle of past performances is included.

700. Piotrowski, Z. "O zastowaniu Komputerow w muzyce mowi Lejaren Hiller." *Ruch Muzycny* 18, 4 (1974), 3-4.

Interview with Hiller.

701. Pittman, Tom; and Bob Davis. A variable architecture computing machine. Proceedings of the West Coast Computer Faire, 1977.

A low-cost computer design which is microprogrammable, relatively high-speed, and available with variable word-widths, was presented at this meeting for home and hobby computing. The machine (named VACuuM) may possibly be very useful to musicians and is described in detail here. See Snell (#857).

702. Plitnik, G.; and W. Strong. "Digital filter techniques for synthesis of bassoon tones." *Journal of the Acoustical Society of America* 47, 1- part 1 (Jan. 1970), 131. Abstract.

Two digital filters, having independent amplitude control, are used to approximate the spectral envelope of the bassoon. Examples of synthetic bassoon tones are available.

703. Pohlman, Ken. See Beauchamp, Pohlman, and Chapman.

704. Poli, Giovanni de. Musica, programme de codage
de la musique. Centre Georges Pompidou
Rapports IRCAM No. 7, Paris, 1978.

Users' manual for an input language for
conventional music scores, with provision
for phrasing and ornamentation.

705. _____; and Giovanni Debiasi. Musica: a
language for transcription of musical texts
for computers. Paper presented at the First
International Conference on Computer Music,
Massachussetts Institute of Technology,
Oct. 28-31, 1976.

The rules for transcribing musical texts
written in conventional notation into data
input for computers are given here. This
system has been used for musicological and
theoretical research, as a teaching aid for
composition, and as a creative tool in the
production of original works.

706. Popplewell, Cicely M., ed. *Information Processing 1962: Proceedings of the IFIP Congress
62.* Amsterdam: North Holland, 1962. 780 pp.

Includes an article by A. W. Slawson.

707. Portnoy, Julius. *Music in the Life of Man.*
New York: Holt, Rinehart, and Winston, 1963.
171-181.

Aesthetic considerations in the use of
computers in music-making are discussed.

708. Potter, Gary M. The role of chance in contemporary music. Diss., Indiana University, 1971.
185 pp. *UM 71-29585.* *Dissertation Abstracts*
32 (1971-72), 5273-A.

Included in this survey are descriptions
of 'stochastic' or probabilistic procedures
used within composition programs.

709. Pousseur, Henri. *Fragments théoretiques sur la
musique expérimentale*. Brussels: Editions
de l'Institut de Sociologie de l'Université
Libre de Bruxelles, 1970.

Many theories of modern musical thought are
discussed here. A special point is made of
the distinction between music utilizing
random processes and stochastic music. There
is also a section on the development of
electronic music through the application
of computers.

710. Powell, Roger. Using the microcomputer as a
multichannel compositionally oriented
controlled-voltage sequencer for synthesizers. Paper presented at the 60th convention of the Audio Engineering Society,
Los Angeles, May 2-5, 1978.

A microprocessor is used here to feed
sequences of data to multiple channels
of an analog synthesizer. The software
provides music editing and such features
as transposition, repeats, and juxtaposi-
tion of sequences. Taped examples were
presented.

711. Powner, E.T.; D.H. Green; and G.T. Taylor.
"Digital waveform synthesis." *Electronic
Engineering* 41, 2 (Aug. 1969), 50-54.

A digital waveform generator which produces
non-standard waveforms as well as sinewaves
is described here.

712. Prieberg, Fred K. *Musica ex Machina.* Berlin:
Verlag Ullstein, 1960. 300 pp.

A historical account of computer music
developments is given.

713. Pruett, James. "The Harpur College Music-Computer
Seminar: a report." *Computers and the Humanities* (1966), 34-38.

A complete report is given on a seminar
which offered instruction in the computer
languages FORTRAN, SNOBOL, and DARMS to
musicians.

714. Pulfer, James K. "Computer aid for musical
composers." *Bulletin of Radio and Electrical
Engineering Division* 20, 2 (1970), 44-48.

715. _____. The computer as an aid to the
composition and production of commercial
music. Paper presented to the 42nd convention of the Audio Engineering Society,
Los Angeles, May 2-5, 1972.

The use of an experimental computer facility
by this member of the National Research
Council of Canada for the production of music
for radio, television and films is described.
Examples of the music and a short film were
presented.

716. _____. "Man-machine interaction in creative
applications." *International Journal of
Man-Machine Studies* 3 (1971), 1-11.

Some aspects of creative activity are reviewed
and means by which the processes involved may
be augmented by the use of computers are outlined. A facility utilizing a SEL 840A computer (16K, 24 bits) for producing simple

musical compositions is described.

717. Pulkert, Oldřich. "Hudba samočinné počitače a jiné novinky." *Hudebnî věda* 4 (1967), 479-484.

718. Quijano, Jean-Pierre. "Musique et ordinateurs électroniques." *Vie Musicale* 16 (June 1970), 21-25.

719. Radaur, Irmfried. "Computer-Komposition." *Melos* 41, 5 (Sept.-Oct. 1974), 278-286.

The necessary considerations in writing a computer program for music composition are discussed. A subprogram for Mathews' MUSIC V program, MUPRO 5, is described in detail. Permutations of tone rows, transposition, and various rhythmic procedures are written into the subprogram; also, notation of tempered-scale pitches and octaves is provided.

720. Rader, G.M. An algorithm for the automatic composition of simple forms of music based on a variation of formal grammars. Moore School Report No. 73-09, University of Pennsylvania, 1973. 98 pp.

721. _____. The formal composition of music. Technical Report No. 77-1, Dept. of Computer Science, University of Ife, Nigeria, 1977.

722. _____. "A method for composing simple traditional music by computer." *Communications of the Association for Computing Machinery* 17, 11 (Nov. 1974), 631-638.

Reprinted in *Computational Musicology Newsletter* 2, 1 (March 1975), 14.

723. Rakowski, Andrzy. "O zastowaniu cyfrowych maszyn matematycznych do muzyki." *Muzka Kwartalnik* 7, 3 (1962), 83-95.

Mathematical approaches to the composition of music are described.

724. Randall, J.K. "'New sounds' vs. musical articulation." *Journal of the Audio Engineering Society* 15, 1 (1967), 96. Abstract.

The interaction of electronic media and musical ideas is discussed and the author puts forth his own position as a composer: it is not a repertoire of 'new sounds' that concerns him, but kinds of relationships needed to articulate some musical structure.

725. _____. "A report from Princeton." *Perspectives of New Music* 3, 2 (1965), 84-92.

An account is given of the use of Bell Laboratories' music program, MUSIC IV, with Princeton's IBM 7094 computer.

726. _____. "Theories of musical structure as a source for problems in psychoacoustical research." *Journal of the Acoustical Society of America* 39, 6 (1966), 1245.

727. _____. "Three lectures to scientists." *Perspectives of New Music* 5, 2 (1967), 124-140.

Portions of this article and those above reprinted as "Two lectures to scientists. Theories of musical structure as a source for problems in psychoacoustical research: 'new sounds' vs. musical articulation." In *Perspectives on Comtemporary Music,* ed. B. Boretz and E. Cone. New York: Norton, 1972. 116-126.

Randall, continued

> The third of the "Three lectures to
> scientists" reprinted as "Operations on
> waveforms" in *Music by Computers*, ed.
> H. von Foerster and J.W. Beauchamp.
> New York: Wiley and Sons, 1969. 122-128.

> The use of the computer as a control for
> the more subtle parameters of sound for
> new possibilities of compositional struc-
> ture is discussed. Of particular interest
> to the composer are operations on sets of
> partials, for which he has designed sub-
> routines to be used with the MUSIC IV music
> program of M. Mathews. The importance of
> musical structure as the overriding concern
> of the composer is emphasized, as opposed
> to novelties in sound.

728. Ranta, M.W. "The avant-garde scene: 'Piece for
     Jazz-Set.'" *Percussionist* 6, 1 (1968),
     13-20.

> The composer summarizes his compositional
> techniques used in a computer-generated
> score for jazz set. The entire score,
> transcribed from print-outs, is reproduced.

729. Reeves, William. See Buxton, Reeves, Baecker,
     and Mezer.

730. Regener, Eric. *Pitch Notation and Equal Tempera-
     ment: A Formal Study*. Occasional Papers
     No. 6. University of California Press, 1973.

731. Régnier, Francis. "Situation de la recherche
     musicale face à la révolution informatique."
     Electronic Music Reports 4 (Sept. 1971),
     8-29.

> The suitability to the present musical
> situation of computer sound synthesis is

compared to that of score generation. A
broad outline of MUSIC V is given and a
general program of sound synthesis for
purposes of musical research and composition
is discussed.

732. Reichardt, Jasia, ed. *Cybernetic Serendipity*.
New York: Praeger, 1969; London: McKay, 1968.
101 pp.

This collection of essays on the computer
and the arts includes reports on specific
projects in this area and reflections on
the theoretic/philosophical basis for such
activities. Contributors include J.R. Pierce,
Stockhausen, J. Tenney, L. Hiller, John Cage,
G. Strang, P. Zinovieff, and T.H. O'Beirne.
See Pierce, Tenney, Hiller, Strang, Zinovieff,
O'Beirne (those most narrowly concerned with
computers and musical composition here).

733. _____. *Cybernetics, Art, and Ideas*. London:
Studio Vista, 1971; Greenwich, Ct.: New York
Graphic Society, 1971. 207 pp.

Includes articles by Iannis Xenakis, Andre
Moles, and Gordon Pask concerning uses of
computers in music-making.

734. Richard, Albert. "Iannis Xenakis." *La Revue Musicale*
257 (1963), 7-8.

Short evaluation of the work of Xenakis.

735. _____. "Interrogatoire d'un musicien."
La Revue Musicale 268-269 (1971), 31-35.

Also, as "Interrogatory of a musician."
Music and Technology. Paris: La Revue Musicale,
1971. 33-38.

Reflections on the nature of 'mechanized music' are presented in the form of a dialogue.

736. Riotti, André. "Informatique musicale: jonction nouvelle entre art et science." *Euro-Spectra* 13, 1 (March 1974), 2-15.

The role of the computer in musical composition and musicological analysis is examined. Musical excerpts, bibliography, and a discography are included.

737. Risset, Jean-Claude. Computer study of trumpet tones. Bell Telephone Laboratories Internal Report, Murray Hill, N.J., 1966. 40 pp.

Also, in *Journal of the Acoustical Society* 38, 5 (Nov. 1965), 912. Abstract.

Trumpet tone quality is studied through analysis and resynthesis by means of a high speed computer. The attack time (varying with each harmonic), fluctuation of pitch frequency, and the harmonic content (which varies with increase in loudness) are determined to be very important.

738. _____. Hauteur et timbre des sons. Centre Georges Pompidou Rapports IRCAM No. 11, 1978.

The implications for theories of hearing of some of the known data on pitch and timbre are discussed, with some examples from psychoacoustical studies and from musical experience. Cassette of recorded examples included.

739. _____. *An Introductory Catalogue of Computer Synthesized Sounds*. Murray Hill, N.J.: Bell Telephone Laboratories, 1969.

Several new unit generators added to Mathews' MUSIC V system are described, followed by diagrams, descriptions, and programs for instrument-like and non-instrument-like sounds, plus descriptions of the physical structure of the results. A recording is included, with examples of sounds and musical phrases.

Reviewed by J.W. Beauchamp, in *Perspectives of New Music* 9, 2/ 10, 1 (Fall-Winter 1971), 348-350.

740. _____. "Music performed by the computer." *Computational Musicology Newsletter* 1, 1 (Oct. 1973), 9.

741. _____. Musical acoustics. Centre Georges Pompidou Rapports IRCAM No. 8, Paris, 1978.

Survey of many of the aspects of musical acoustics, beginning with a discussion of pitch, duration, and rhythm, then the physics and timbres of musical instruments, ending with synthetic and electronic music.

742. _____. "L'ordinateur, instrument de musique." *Conférences des Journées d'Etudes du Festival International du Son Haute Fidelité Stereophonie*. Paris: Editions Chiron, 1970. 150-159.

Also, in *Revue d'Acoustique* 4, 16 (1971), 286-290.

The process of sound synthesis by means
of computers is explained and some of
the resulting sounds are described. The
author proposes that a new relationship
between pitch and frequency might be
found. Illustrations, bibliography,
and discography included.

743. _____. Paradoxes de hauteur. Centre
Georges Pompidou Rapports IRCAM No. 10,
Paris, 1978.

Following up on the investigation of
Shepard's tones (seemingly endlessly
descending glissandi), new and different
'paradoxical' sounds have been produced:
sounds that appear to slow down while
actually speeding up. Some discussion
of the implications for a theory of
hearing is included. Cassette of
recorded examples accompanies the
report.

744. _____. Pitch control and pitch paradoxes
demonstrated with computer-synthesized
sounds. Paper presented to the 77th
meeting of the American Acoustical
Society, 1969.

Also, in *Journal of the Acoustical
Society of America* 46, 1, 1 (1969), 88.
Abstract.

Unusual sounds created by manipulating
overtones in computer-synthesized tones,
such as seemingly endlessly descending
glissandi (Shepard's tones), sequences
perceived as descending although the
final pitch is perceived as higher, and
other effects are described.

745. _____. "Quelques remarques sur les musiques pour ordinateur et l'interprétation." *Musique en jeu* 3 (1971), 5-11.

Possible applications of the computer in performance are examined: determination of a completed version of partly aleatory scores or sound synthesis in live performance, versus compositions stored on magnetic tape.

746. _____. Sur l'analyse, la synthèse, et la perception des sons étudies à l'aide de calculateurs électroniques. Diss., Orsay, 1967.

747. _____. "Synthèse des sons musicaux à l'aide des calculateurs électronique." *Conférences des Journées d'Etudes du Festival Internaional du Son.* Paris: Editions Chiron, 1966. 93.

Summary of work on digital synthesis of instrument tones carried out by the author.

748. _____. "Synthèse des sons à l'aide d'ordinateurs." *La Revue Musicale* 268-269 (1971), 112-123.

Also, as "Synthesis of sounds by computer and problems concerning timbre." *Music and Technology.* Paris: La Revue Musicale, 1971. 117-128.

A description is offered of sound generation using the MUSIC V system and 'paradoxical' sounds obtained by computer synthesis, with resulting conclusions on perception.

177

749. _____; Gerard Charbonneau; and
P. Karantchentzeff. "Un system de
synthèse directe des sons à l'aide
d'ordinateurs." *Revue d'Acoustique*
21 (1972), 289-296.

750. _____; Max V. Mathews. "Analysis of musical
instrument tones." *Physics Today* 22, 2
(Feb. 1969), 23-30.

Descriptions are given of techniques for
analyzing tone quality of trumpet and
violin tones. Simulated tones were then
produced by means of computed sound synthesis. This has led to the discovery
of other factors besides the relative
amounts of various harmonics present
simultaneously which are pertinent to
tone quality. The use of the computer
itself as a musical instrument is mentioned and the use of information gained
from these researches in going beyond the
classes of sounds of traditional musical
instruments is speculated upon.

751. _____. See Gardner, Harvey, Lawson, Risset.

752. _____. See Mathews, Moore, Risset.

753. _____. See Mathews, Pierce, Risset.

754. _____. See Mathews, Miller, Pierce, Moore,
and Risset.

755. Rittenbach, Bruce. Aspects of computer music
system design. Paper presented to the
First International Conference on Computer
Music, Massachussetts Institute of Technology, Oct. 28-31, 1976.

The distinction between sound generating
systems and musical structure generating
systems is explored here. Related topics
such as process hierarchies, distributed
intelligence, musical time vs. sample time,
and generality vs. the system-as-a-composition
are discussed.

756. Roads, Curtis. "Automated granular synthesis of
sound." *Computer Music Journal* 2, 2
(Sept. 1978), 61.

The author describes a technique of digital
sound synthesis based on the ideas of Xenakis
and Moles, which produces a different class
of sounds from the more usual techniques. It
is implemented as a front-end processor
interfaced to a MUSIC V program at a Burroughs
B6700 installation. Events are formed as
conglomerates of short bursts of sound. It
is suggested that this method could be adapted
for digital synthesizers such as those of
Alles and Samson.

757. _____. "An interview with Gottfried Michael
Koenig." *Computer Music Journal* 2, 3
(Dec. 1978), 11-15.

The composer's early development, involvement
in electronic music during the 50's, first
experiences with computer programming, PROJECT
1 and 2, opinions on digital synthesizers,
and the Institute of Sonology are discussed.

758. _____. "Magazine review: *Faire*." *Computer
Music Journal* 2, 3 (Dec. 1978), 10.

Review of a publication released by the
Groupe de Musique Experimentale de Bourges
in France, which includes articles relevant
to the use of computers in music.

759. _____. "A report on the 1978 International
Computer Music Conference." *Computer
Music Journal* 2, 4 (Dec. 1978), 21-27.

Report on papers, demonstrations, and
concerts given at a conference held at
Northwestern University, Evanston, Ill.,
Nov. 1-5, 1978. Photographs included.

760. _____. "The UNESCO workshop on computer
music at Aarhus, Denmark." *Computer
Music Journal* 2, 3 (Dec. 1978), 30-32.

Account of activities, lectures, and
concerts during this workshop, held at
The Institute of Musicology, Aug. 28-Sept.
1, 1978.

761. Roberts, Arthur. An all-FORTRAN music-generating
computer program. Paper presented at the
17th convention of the Audio Engineering
Society, New York, Oct. 11-15, 1965.

Also, in *Journal of the Audio Engineering
Society* 14, 1 (Jan. 1966), 17-20.

Description is given of an adaptation of
Mathews' MUSIC IV program to 3600 FORTRAN.
An ASI-210 was used for D/A conversion at
Argonne National Laboratory. Flow-charts
of the MUSIC 4F program are included.

762. _____. "Some new developments in computer-
generated music." In *Music by Computers*,
ed. H. von Foerster and J.W. Beauchamp.
New York: Wiley and Sons, 1969. 63-68.

Description of a FORTRAN program developed
at Argonne National Laboratories, formerly
called MUSIC 4F and renamed ORPHEUS, as it
has come to diverge considerably from its

parent program MUSIC IV. The major change
is that 'instruments' are not assembled
each time the program is run; instead, there
is one instrument which is made available to
all individual voices and includes all the
resources of the program. *Sonatina for
CDC-3600*, a composition programmed by the
author, is described and included in a recording which accompanies the book.

763. _____. "Some notes on computer-generated
music." *Journal of the Acoustical Society
of America* 39, 6 (June 1966), 1245-1246.
Abstract.

This paper deals with the use of MUSIC 4F
and improvement of the linear-amplitude
characteristics of 'instruments' generated
by the computer.

764. Rogers, Bruce. "The Center for Studies in Mathe-
matical and Automated Music, Paris (CEMAMu)."
Numus-West [Mercer Island, Washington] 4
(April 1973), 6-10.

An outline of teaching activities, research
in acoustics and light as related to music,
and composition of instrumental, electro-
acoustic, and mixed media works is given.
Xenakis work for magnetic tape and lasers,
Polytope de Cluny, is also described.

765. _____. A user's manual for the stochastic
music program. Bloomington, Ind., 1972.

Manual for the free stochastic program used
by Xenakis at Indiana University, described
in Xenakis' book, *Formalized Music*.

766. Rogers, John. "Some properties of non-duplicating rotational arrays." *Perspectives of New Music* 7, 1 (Fall-Winter 1968), 80-102.

A particular type of pitch structure which is similar to those used in the later music of Stravinsky and Krenek is developed here. A program has been written by the author and Myron Curtis at Bowdoin College to generate complete listings of all possible permutations of pitch sets which exhibit the specified characteristics. Some suggestions for compositional use are presented. A serial method employing 19 equal-tempered divisions of the octave, with waveforms generated by the MUSIC IV system is mentioned as the ongoing work of the author. Scores are also included.

767. _____. "Toward a system of rotational arrays." *Proceedings of the American Society of University Composers* 2 (1969), 61-74.

Search programs for solving musical problems involving the use of rotational arrays are discussed. The use of these programs for structuring linear and vertical sets for a 19-tone division of the octave is suggested as a possibility.

768. _____. "The uses of digital computers in electronic music." In *The Development and Practice of Electronic Music,* ed. Jon Appleton and Ronald Perera. Englewood Cliffs, N.J.: Prentice-Hall, 1975. 189-285.

General discussion of features and problems of all computer programs for music, but in particular, 4B-type programs. MUSIC 360 is also described. Bibliography and discography are provided.

769. Rogers, M. "Performing the sound of one hand clapping (computerized digital synthesizer)." *Rolling Stone* 206 (Feb. 12, 1976), 46-47.

770. Rolnick, Neil B. "A composer's notes on the development and implementation of software for a digital synthesizer." *Computer Music Journal* 2, 2 (Sept. 1978), 13-22.

Discussion of problems encountered in the design and implementation of SYN4B, a programming language for use with the 4B digital synthesizer. This system employs a LSI-11/03 microprocessor and was designed and built by G. diGiugno and H.G. Alles at the Institut de Recherche et Coordination Acoustique/Musique in Paris. The language for the system was written by Phillippe Prevot and the author.

771. Rosenboom, David. Homuncular homophony. Unpublished paper, 1971.

772. _____. "In support of a systems theoretical approach to art media." *Proceedings of the American Society of University Composers* 5 (1970), 56-68.

Apologia for the use of technology by artists and description of the author's own recent projects, including the building of a briefcase-size computer synthesizer and a live-performance composing studio.

773. _____. "A model for detection and analysis of information processing modalities in the nervous system through an adaptive, interactive, computerized electronic music instrument." In *Information Processing Systems,* Proceedings of the Second Annual Music Computation Conference, Nov. 7-9, 1975, part 4. Urbana:

University of Illinois, 1975. 54-78.

Reprinted from *Biofeedback and the Arts:
Results of Early Experiments,* ed. David
Rosenboom. 2nd ed. Vancouver, B.C.:
Aesthetic Research Center, 1975.

A laboratory for investigating brain
activity in relation to aesthetic experience at York University, established in
1972, is described. Results of various
experiments and artistic activities are
related, with conclusions drawn as to the
functioning of the brain under musical
stimuli and neural information processing.
A new research and performance instrument
is being developed as an extension of these
conclusions, making use of a computer and
synthesis system.

774. Rosenstein, Milton. "Computer-generated pure tones
and noise and its application to psychoacoustics." *Journal of the Audio Engineering Society* 21, 2 (March 1973), 121-126.

Also, presented at the 43rd convention of
the Audio Engineering Society, New York,
Sept. 12-15, 1972. Preprint No. 882 K-2.

Digital sound generation is used to test
levels of human detection, which has been
found to depend on pattern differences as
well as intensity ratios between noise and
tone.

775. Rosler, Lawrence. The Graphic-1 7094 Graphical
Interaction System and the GRIN94 Language.
Murray Hill, N.J.: Bell Telephone Labora-
tories, n.d.

User's manual and research report.

776. _____. See Mathews and Rosler.

777. Rossum, David. "Some thoughts on microprocessors in music." *Computer Music Journal* 1, 2 (April 1977), 62-63.

This article is directed to home computer enthusiasts, suggesting the use of micro-computers as controllers for analog equipment, which may be built by the hobbyist himself from published designs or purchased building block circuits (such as those made by Eμ Systems, with whom the author is associated). Advice on construction of the interface is given.

778. _____; and Scott Wedge. A microprocessor-based polyphonic keyboard for modular electronic music systems. Paper presented to the 57th convention of the Audio Engineering Society, Los Angeles, May 10-13, 1977. Preprint No. 1231.

The system described includes a single board hardware configuration interfaced with a keyboard, user controls, 16 channels of analog input, and tape output to the central processing unit. Dual section keyboard use and sequencer functions are available.

779. Rothenberg, David. A language for musical composition and analysis. Unpublished paper, Rutgers University, 1974.

780. _____. "A non-procedural language for musical composition." In *Composition with Computers*, Proceedings of the Second Annual Music Computation Conference, Nov. 7-9, 1975, part 2. Urbana: University of Illinois, 1975. 37-67.

A language by which a composition may be
described and more or less narrowly defined
for realization by means of computers is
outlined. A hybrid synthesizer with keyboard controllers and a score printer has
been used to produce several different
versions from a given compositional description.

781. _____. A topological model for the perception of context-embedded materials. Paper
presented at the First International Conference on Computer Music, Massachussetts
Institute of Technology, Oct. 28-31, 1976.

Possible relations between musical sequences
of timbres analogous to those which apply
to sequences of pitch (transposition,
extension, modal sequence) are considered
here. Applications to the development of
new materials for 'tone-color music' are
proposed and appropriate hardware for
producing these materials is described.

782. Roy, John. "A digital sound synthesizer." In
*Hardware for Computer-Controlled Sound
Synthesis*, Proceedings of the Second Annual
Music Computation Conference, Nov. 7-9.
1975, part 4. Urbana: University of Illinois,
1975. 49-57.

Description of a digital synthesizer to be
interfaced with a PDP-11/10 minicomputer
being developed as part of a computer arts
studio at the University of Massachussetts
with the aim of interaction between music
and visual arts. The system may also be
used as a video image generator.

783. Rush, Loren; and James A. Moorer. Editing, mixing, and processing digitized audio waveforms. Paper presented at the 57th convention of the Audio Engineering Society, Los Angeles, May 10-13, 1977.

An interactive computer-based system at Stanford University for editing, mixing, and processing digitized waveforms is described. Various techniques for manipulating data, and recorded examples, were presented.

784. _____; _____; and Gareth Loy. All digital sound recording and processing. Paper presented at the 55th convention of the Audio Engineering Society, Oct. 29, 1976.

Techniques of high quality sound recording via D/A converter and files of the digitized sound are described, with further processing of these files a possibility. Examples, produced at the Center for Computer Research in Music and Acoustics at Stanford University, were presented.

785. _____. See Chowning, Grey, Moorer, Rush.

786. Ruiz, Pierre. Technique for simulating the vibrations of strings with a digital computer. Thesis, University of Illinois, 1970.

787. _____. See Hiller and Ruiz.

788. Rytvinsskaya, M.S. See Bukharaev and Rytvinsskaya.

789. Sadie, S. "New music." *Musical Times* 109 (March 1968), 252.

Two compositions employing computers, *December Quartet* and *Partita for unattended computer* by Peter Zinovieff, are briefly reviewed.

790. Samson, Peter. Systems Concepts Digital Synthesizer specifications. San Francisco, Cal.,
1977. Available from Systems Concepts,
520 Third St., San Francisco, Cal., U.S.A.

Technical description of the author's
real-time digital synthesizer, which was
one of the first of this type.

791. _____; and R. Clements. "Music systems for
the PDP-10." *DECUS* [Maynard, Mass.: Digital
Equipment Corporation] 10, 9 (April 1973),
n.p.

792. Sankiewicz, M. See Budzynski and Sankiewicz.

793. Saripov, R. "Musik und Rechenautomat." *Ideen
des exakten Wissens* 2 (1969), 71-77.

Aesthetic considerations in the employ of
computers in music-making are debated.

794. Sasaki, L. See Buxton, Fogels, Federkow, Sasaki,
and Smith.

795. Saunders, Steven. "Improved FM audio synthesis
methods for real-time digital music generation." *Computer Music Journal* 1, 1
(Feb. 1977), 53-55.

Description of a variation on Chowning's
frequency modulation technique using a
triangle-wave modulating signal, implemented
for real-time generation on a minicomputer
with D/A converter.

796. _____. "Real-time digital FM audio synthesis."
In *Software Synthesis Techniques*, Proceedings
of the Second Annual Music Computation Conference, Nov. 7-9, 1975, part 1. Urbana:
University of Illinois, 1975. 42-52.

A form of frequency modulation synthesis
using a triangle-wave modulating signal is
described. This software technique was intended for economical, real-time sound
generation on a digital synthesizer (called
'Twang') developed at the Xerox Palo Alto
Research Center. See also, T. Kaehler,
"Some music at Xerox PARC," for more on this
project.

797. Schaeffer, Pierre. "De l'expérience musicale à
l'expérience humaine." *La Revue Musicale*
274-275 (1971), 1-163. (Entire issue).

This issue is entirely devoted to the thinking
of Pierre Schaeffer. Interviews and speeches
are interspersed with essays on philosophy
and aesthetics. The second section includes
an essay specifically on computer music,
"A-propos des ordinateurs."

798. _____. "La musique et les ordinateurs."
La Revue Musicale 268-269 (1971), 57-88.

Also, as "Music and computers." *Music and
Technology*. Paris: La Revue Musicale, 1971.
57-92.

The value of intuition as well as computer
calculation is emphasized, and the simulation
of mental processes of the composer, formal
musics, the ideas of Knut Wiggen and Milton
Babbitt, sound generation, and musical grammar
are subjects for comment.

799. Schafer, R.W.   Principles of digital signal
        processing.   Paper presented to the 41st
        convention of the Audio Engineering Soc-
        iety, New York, Oct. 5-8, 1971.

        Principles of techniques that are useful
        in processing audio signals are presented.
        Topics include recursive digital filters,
        finite duration impulse response filters,
        and discrete Fourier transform (all of
        which are applicable to digital sound
        generation).

800. Schappert, H.   See Neumann and Schappert.

801. Schat, Peter. "The dream of reason-- the reason
        of a dream." *Keynotes: Musical Life in
        the Netherlands* [Amsterdam: Donemus] 2
        (1976), 39-47.

        Objections of a conservative composer to
        the use of computers in composition.

802. Scherpenisse, J. "Digital control in electronic
        music studios." *Interface* 6, 2 (Sept.
        1977), 73-80.

        Also, presented to the 56th convention of
        the Audio Engineering Society, Paris,
        March 1-4, 1977.   Preprint No. 1195.

        A proposal is made here for an electronic
        music studio featuring manual control,
        voltage control, and digital control. A
        digital bus system and a microcomputer
        would form the heart of the system.

803. _____.   See Tempelaars and Scherpenisse.

804. Schiffer, B. "Athens." *Music and Musicians* 24 (Dec. 1975), 60-61.

Description of new music by Greek composers; particularly, the new works of I. Xenakis.

805. Schottstaedt, Bill. "The simulation of natural instrument tones using frequency modulation with a complex modulating wave." *Computer Music Journal* 1, 4 (Nov. 1977), 46-50.

An elaboration of Chowning's frequency modulation technique for creating complex audio spectra digitallly is described here. By using complex modulating waves made up of two or three sinusoids, string and piano tones have been simulated. This technique is seen to offer unexplored potential.

806. Schwartz, Elliott. *Electronic Music: A Listener's Guide.* New York: Praeger, 1973. 87-101.

In a chapter on computer-generated sound, a thorough introduction to the subject is given, covering the work of Hiller and Isaacson, Mathews, Tenney, Randall, Howe, Winham, Cage, Dodge, Vercoe, and Risset. Facilities used and music produced are discussed.

807. Seay, Albert. "The composer and the computer." *Computers and Automation* 13, 8 (Aug. 1964), 16-18.

808. Sedelow, Sally Yeates. "The computer in the humanities and fine arts." *Computing Surveys* 2, 2 (1970), 89-110.

Discussion of pattern recognition and analysis in the arts and pattern construction as the kind of tasks for which humanists are seeking computer assistance. The problems posed by

these tasks for data representation and
manipulation are pointed out for the
benefit of other computer scientists.
L. Hiller's work is mentioned.

809. Seifert, Wolfgang. "Über Musik und zum Computer."
Neue Zeitschrift für Musik 133 (1972),
104-106.

Review of H. Brün's book, *Über Musik und
zum Computer.*

810. Selleck, John. "Computer partitioning."
*Proceedings of the American Society of
University Composers* 7-8 (1972-73),
90-110.

The computer is used to perform pre-compo-
sitional calculation of 'set partitions'
based on the serial technique. Program
and diagrams are included.

811. Shanks, J.L.   See Justice and Shanks.

812. Shapero, Harold. "Remarks." *Proceedings of the
American Society of University Composers*
1 (1968), 54-55.

Speculations on the likelihood of lyricism
in computer music.

813. Shaw, Jane A. "Computers and the humanities."
Electronic Age 24, 2 (Spring 1965),
26-29.

814. Shibata, Minao. "Musique et technologie au
Japon." *La Revue Musicale* 268-269 (1971),
173-180.

Also, as "Music and technology in Japan."
Music and Technology. Paris: La Revue

Musicale, 1971. 173-180.

The development of electronic music in
Japan is described and works by Japanese
composers cited.

815. Shima, Kenji. See Hibino and Shima.

816. Sierad, T. "Tune in some chips." *Byte* 2, 9
(Sept. 1977), 84-95.

Outline for a programmable tone generator
to be constructed from a few IC's, resistors,
capacitors, and prototyping board and used
with a microcomputer.

817. Sigurbjornson, Thörkel. "Introduction to the
HYBRID IV working." *Faire* [Bourges:
Editions GMEB] 4/5 (May 1978), 10.

Report on the author's experiences at the
Center for Music Experiment in La Jolla, Cal.,
where he worked with Ed Kobrin's HYBRID IV
system.

818. Silverman, Faye-Ellen. "Report from New York City:
Computer Conference, June 1973." *Current
Musicology* 17 (1974), 77-80.

Report on a conference on the use of the
computer in music, art, and film.

819. Silverston, Stefan; and Gary White. "Report on
the Iowa State computerized music system."
Numus West [Mercer Island, Washington]
2, 1 (Winter 1975), 32-37.

A hybrid system including a PDP 11/10 computer and a Buchla synthesizer, under development at Iowa State University for two
years, is described. Compositions and teaching

193

materials are described and the interface language is explained in some detail.

820. _____. See White, Smay, and Silverston.

821. Simon, Herbert A.; and R.K. Summer. "Pattern in music." In *Formal Representation of Human Judgement*, ed. B. Kleinmuntz. New York: Wiley, 1968. 219-250.

Complex information processing under musical stimulation is considered, with research in the field of artificial intelligence being applied to musical activities.

822. Sims, Greg. Applications of air-pressure transducers in digitally synthesized sound. Paper presented at the 60th convention of the Audio Engineering Society, Los Angeles, May 2-5, 1978.

A hybrid IC pressure transducer has been interfaced to the Alles digital synthesizer at Bell Laboratories for event triggering and continuous parameter control.

823. _____. Enhancement of synthetic sounds by dynamic parameter reverberation. Paper presented at the 60th convention of the Audio Engineering Society, Los Angeles, May 2-5, 1978.

A method of dynamically varying 'room' reverberators (using the Schroeder-Logan algorithm) was implemented on the Alles digital sound synthesizer in order to reproduce some of the interesting, natural irregularities of acoustic sounds.

824. Sittner, Hans. "Technische Medien im Dienst der
     Musik." *Österreichische Musikzeitschrift*
     23 (1968), 121-122.

     Overview of the uses of new technology in
     music, including the computer.

825. "Situation de la musique électroacoustique en
     5 themes: musique et machines." *Faire*
     [Bourges: Editions GMEB] 2/3 (1974), 183-206.

     Discussion including Leo Kupper, W. Buxton,
     P. Pignon, P. Menard, W. Kotonski, P. Clozier,
     P. Boeswillwald, J. Appleton, A. Savouret,
     and C. Aharonian.

826. Skolyszewski, Franciszek. "Dotychczasowe próby
     zastosowań cybernetyki do muzyki." *Muzyka*
     11, 3-4 (1966), 36-63.

827. Slawson, A. Wayne. "Computer applications in music."
     Journal of Music Theory 12 (1968), 205-211.

     Review of *Papers from the West Virginia
     Conference,* ed. by G. Lefkoff.

828. _____. Input languages affect system design.
     Paper read at the First International Con-
     ference on Computer Music, Massachussetts
     Institute of Technology, Oct. 28-31, 1976.

     The author's SYNTAL program is described as
     a powerful tool for use with small computers
     and tight budgets. Advantages include com-
     poser-defined nested 'macro' and repetition
     features which make it possible to specify
     music in a program-like form and to imple-
     ment variation, transformation, and develop-
     ment in a straight-forward manner.

195

829. _____. "MUSE-- a sound synthesizer." In
*Information Processing 1962: Proceedings
of the IFIP Congress 62*, ed. Cicely M.
Popplewell. Amsterdam: North Holland, 1963.
451-455.

Description of a program written for an
IBM 7090 computer. The program statements
give data in terms of spectrum number, time,
and fundamental frequency with amplitude
multiplier, and the frequencies and band-
widths of up to ten resonances.

830. _____. "A speech-oriented synthesizer of
computer music." *Journal of Music Theory*
13, 1 (1969), 94-127.

A description of the programs, as they
existed at Yale University in June 1966,
which were intended to exploit sounds of
speech musically is given. The specification language, with examples of coding, and
synthesizer operation are outlined. Function
tables employed by the author in his work
Movements for Orchestra with Tape are
included.

831. _____. "Vowel quality and musical timbre as
functions of spectrum envelope and fundamental frequency." *Journal of the Acoustical Society of America* 43, 1 (1968), 87-
101.

Judgements made by observers determined that
the two lower formants made large differences
in vowel quality and musical timbre. Other
variations in spectrum envelopes of vowel
sounds and musical timbres were carried out
also, using the 'buzz-generator' of a speech
synthesizer at Harvard University and at

the Massachussetts Institute of Technology.

832. Slaymaker, F.H. "Chords from tones having stretched partials." *Journal of the Acoustical Society of America* 47, 1- part 1 (Jan. 1970), 132. Abstract.

> The researcher has generated tones by means of a computer and used them to form chords. Tones containing inharmonic partials (made by systematically moving frequencies of partials away from the harmonic series) are formed in chords in such a way that the upper partials do not form beats and are thus consonant but of strange tone quality.

833. Smay, Terry. See White, Smay, and Silverston.

834. Smith, Bennet. See Bernfeld and Smith.

835. _____. See Wessel and Smith.

836. Smith, Dave. A microcomputer-controlled performance synthesizer. Paper presented to the 60th convention of the Audio Engineering Society, Los Angeles, May 2-5,1978.

> The design of a programmable polyphonic synthesizer using a microcomputer and voltage-controllable analog circuitry is discussed. The internal electronic circuitry and the software are examined.

837. Smith, K.C. See Buxton, Fogels, Federkow, Sasaki, and Smith.

838. _____. See Federkow, Buxton, and Smith.

839. Smith, Leland C. "Computer generation of music."
Journal of the Audio Engineering Society
19, 5 (May 1971), 443. Abstract.

Also, presented to the 40th convention of
the Audio Engineering Society, Los Angeles,
May 1971.

Development of a computer language using
computer generated sound systems by means
of principle musical terminology is
discussed. The intent is to provide the
means by which musicians can use the computer as a musical instrument.

840. _____. "Humanization of computer music."
*Journal of the Acoustical Society of
America* 48, 1- part 1 (July 1970), 88.
Abstract.

At the Stanford University computer music
facility it is now possible to enter strict
rhythm data using either real-time values
or musical terminology. A supplementary
program called RHYTHM reads real-time input
from two telegraph keys. The main program,
SCORE, allows for specification of time
points to be coordinated. After the separate
parts are prepared, RHYTHM may be used to
'conduct' the entire piece, thus achieving
some rhythmic flexibility.

841. _____. "SCORE-- a musician's approach to
computer music." *Journal of the Audio
Engineering Society* 20, 1 (Jan.-Feb. 1972),
7-14.

Reprinted in *Numus-West* [Mercer Island,
Washington] 4 (April 1973), 21-28.

A description from the user's point of
view is made of a program called SCORE,
intended to allow the composer easier
communications with the computer so that
he or she may concentrate on musical problems.

842. _____; and John Chowning. "Computer music."
  Computers and the Humanities 4, 5 (May 1970),
  346.

  Abbreviated research report.

843. Smith, Stuart. "Communications." *Perspectives of
  New Music* 11, 2 (Spring-Summer 1973), 269-
  277.

  Discussion of the final chapter of I. Xenakis'
  book *Formalized Music*, in which he proposes
  to generate complex 'microsound contours'
  through stochastic processes. One method of
  doing this, suggested in the book, was tested
  by the author at the University of New Hampshire, employing the university's IBM 360/50
  computer. The results sounded disappointingly
  like white noise, however.

844. _____. "Computer music in 1972." *Computers
  and Automation* 21, 10 (Oct. 1972), 16-17, 42.

  The difficulties of instituting a music-
  generating program are outlined; a short
  description is given of the use of a minicomputer to control an analog synthesizer,
  and the possibilities of digital synthesis
  are projected.

845. Smoliar, Stephen. Basic research in computer
  music studies. Israel Institute of Technology Computer Science Department Technical
  Report No. 20, Haifa, Israel, Oct. 1972.

Reprinted in *Interface* 2, 2 (Dec. 1973), 121-125.

Future applications of the computer as a partner to the musician are discussed, with reference to the author's own program EUTERPE for constructing formal models of musical compositions. Real-time interactive facilities are emphasized.

846. _____. "Comment on Moorer's 'Music and computer composition.'" *Communications of the Association for Computing Machinery* 15 (1972), 1000-1001.

Continued discussion of Moorer's article on generating tunes through statistical processes. Moorer replies to this comment. See also, Moorer (#617 and #621).

847. _____. "A data structure for an interactive music system." *Interface* 2, 2 (Dec. 1973), 127-140.

Also, as Israel Institute of Technology Department of Computer Science Technical Report No. 21, Haifa, Israel, Oct. 1972.

The EUTERPE2 data structure is a representation of a musical score, designed so that it may be manipulated through an on-line interactive system. Language is an extension of the machine language; the program runs on a PDP-15 computing system.

848. _____. EUTERPE: a computer language for the expression of musical ideas. Massachussetts Institute of Technology Project MAC Artificial Intelligence Memo No. 129, Cambridge, Mass., April 1967. Mimeo.

849. _____. EUTERPE-LISP: a LISP system with music output. Massachussetts Institute of Technology Artificial Intelligance Memo No. 141, Cambridge, Mass., Sept. 1967. 16 pp.

850. _____. Music programs and their syntactic aspects; semantic aspects of music programs; sonological aspects of music programs; the interaction of syntax, semantics, and sonology. CIS 580D Lecture Notes. Department of Computer Science, University of Pennsylvania, Philadelphia, Pa., 1974. 42 pp.

851. _____. *A Parallel Processing Model of Musical Structures*. Diss., Massachussetts Institute of Technology, 1971. Springfield, Va.: National Technical Information Service, 1971. Document AD-731690.

Also, as Massachussetts Institute of Technology Project MAC Report No. 91, Cambridge, 1971. 276 pp.

The program EUTERPE, real-time computer system for modeling musical structures, is described in detail. Although applied primarily to musical analysis, speculation is made on the possible use of the system's sound synthesis apparatus for making original compositions.

852. _____. Process structuring and music theory. University of Pennsylvania Moore School of Electrical Engineering Technical Report, Philadelphia, May 1974.

Also, in *Journal of Music Theory* 18, 2 (Fall 1974), 308-336.

Reprinted in *Computational Musicology Newsletter* 2, 1 (March 1975), 17.

853. _____. Systematic aspects of musical
activity. Israel Institute of Technology
Computer Science Department Technical Report No. 28, Haifa, Israel, June 1973.

854. _____. Using the EUTERPE music system.
Massachussetts Institute of Technology
Artificial Intelligence Laboratory Memo
No. 243, Cambridge, Oct. 1971.

855. _____; and M. Joseph Willson. "Proposal
for an interactive computer-music facility."
Numus-West [Mercer Island, Washington]
1, 5 (1974), 39-43.

Also, in *Computational Musicology Newsletter*
2, 1 (March 1975), 5-6.

Description is given of the design of a
proposed system at the University of
Pennsylvania employing a general-purpose
minicomputer as a control device for a
network of digital waveform generators.
Smoliar's previous work on EUTERPE, a
programming language for constructing
formal models of musical compositions,
will be fundamental to the current work.

856. Snell, John. "Design of a digital oscillator
which will generate up to 256 low distortion sine waves in real time." *Computer
Music Journal* 1, 2 (April 1977), 4-25.

Detailed description of a digital oscillator which may be used as part of a musical
instrument or controlled with an inexpensive microprocessor. Envelopes may be
programmed or generated by a hardware
envelope generator (described here) which
will produce up to 256 different envelopes.
Sine summation synthesis and frequency

modulation synthesis with multiple carriers and/or modulators are also possible. The article begins with basic facts of acoustics, sampling theory, frequency resolution, etc. Time multiplexing results in a large quantity of sinusoidal components. Diagrams, graphs included.

857. _____. "Desirable features of an inexpensive computer used for sound synthesis." *Computer Music Journal* 1, 2 (April 1977), 36-38.

Review of inexpensive computers now commercially available. Among those evaluated in terms of word-width and versatility, VACuuM (Variable Architecture Computing Machine) emerges as the best design. Micro-coding in PDP-10 and PDP-11 instruction sets may be used with it, and it may be expanded from 8 bits to 16, 32, or 36 bits, thus emulating word-widths used by DEC, IBM, and many other popular minicomputers and microprocessors. Provision has been made for parallel processing with separate units.

858. _____. "High speed multiplication." *Computer Music Journal* 1, 1 (1977), 38-45.

High speed multiplication is useful for varying the amplitudes of hundreds of partials in real-time. Several different integrated circuits for this purpose are described here. Schematics and charts are included. Spatial movement of sound, digital filtering, and varying the index of modulation in FM synthesis of timbre are a few other uses of multipliers.

859. Sowa, J.R. "A machine to compose music." In
     Geniac Manual. New York: Oliver Eafield,
     1964.

     This was based on Pinkerton's 'banal tune-
     maker' program. The random number generator
     produced materials which were tested against
     rules given in the program.

860. Steiger, Richard. OEDIT-- an interactive orches-
     tra editing system. Paper presented to the
     First International Conference on Computer
     Music, Massachussetts Institute of Technol-
     ogy, Oct. 28-31, 1976.

     OEDIT is an interactive graphical orchestra
     editor for the MUSIC-11 digital synthesis
     system at the MIT Experimental Music Studio.
     Editing is done by drawing on a digitizing
     tablet. Instruments are represented as
     networks of signal processing, timing and
     control elements. Aural feedback is avail-
     able.

861. _____. Very wide dynamic range digital-to-
     audio converters for computer music syn-
     thesis. Paper presented to the 52nd con-
     vention of the Audio Engineering Society,
     New York, Oct. 31-Nov. 3, 1975.

     Description is given of a new D/A converter
     design which extends the usable dynamic
     range to over 100 decibels for increased
     expressive possibility in digital synthesis.

862. Steiglitz, K. See Cann, Lansky, Steiglitz, and
     Zuckerman.

863. _____. See Winham and Steiglitz.

864. _____. See Zuckerman and Steiglitz.

865. Stephan, Rudolph. "Experimentelle Musik."
Österreichische Musikzeitschrift 26 (1971),
522.

Review of F. Winckel's *Experimentelle Musik*.

866. _____, ed. *Die Musik der Sechziger Jahre.
Zwölf Versuche*. Veröffentlichungen des
Instituts für neue Musik und Musikerzeihung
Darmstadt, 12. Mainz: Schott, 1972. 162 pp.

Twelve essays on music of the sixties, including explorations involving the use of
the computer, written by Ulrich Siegele,
Elmar Budd, Hans Oesche, Ulrich Debelius,
Josef Häusler, Reinhold Brinkmann, Carl
Dahlhaus, Ekkehard Jost, Rudolf Stephan,
and Christian Martin Schmidt.

867. Stewart, David. "Circuit: a report." *Perspectives
of New Music* 11, 2 (Spring–Summer 1973),
265–268.

Report on a conference for computer technology in the arts, literature, and music, called
CIRCUIT, held in south-eastern Michigan in
April 1973. A program of computer-generated
music was given continuously on tape in a
gallery containing other types of works
produced by means of computers. Summaries of
papers presented by D. Wessel, J. Clough,
and M. Babbitt are included here.

868. Stockham, T.G., Jr. A/D and D/A converters:
their effect on digital audio fidelity.
Paper presented at the 41st convention of
the Audio Engineering Society, New York,
Oct. 5–8, 1971. Preprint No. 834.

An explanation is offered for distortions
caused by A/D and D/A converters with the

specifications necessary to avoid these.

869. Stockhausen, Karlheinz. "Elektronische Musik und Automatik." *Melos* 32, 10 (1965), 337-344.

The composer gives his opinions of automatic sound composition, including recent work at the University of Illinois and at Bell Laboratories, and then discusses other automatic processes used in electronic music by himself and others in Cologne and elsewhere.

870. Stockman, Erich, ed. *Studia Instrumentorum musicae popularis II.* Stockholm: Musikhistoriska museet, 1972. 196 pp.

Includes article by Per Tjernlund.

871. Stoney, William. "Theoretical possibilities for equally tempered musical systems." In *The Computer and Music,* ed. Harry B. Lincoln. Ithaca: Cornell University Press, 1970. 163-171.

Analysis of temperaments used by Helmholtz, Mandelbaum, and others is first offered. A program is then described for investigating the characteristics of 12 to 144 equal divisions of the octave, using digital sound synthesis.

872. Strang, Gerald. "The computer in musical composition." *Computers and Automation* 15, 8 (Aug. 1966), 16-17.

Also, in *Cybernetic Serendipity*, ed. Jasia Reichardt. New York: Praeger, 1969. 26-28.

A brief introduction to computer music.

873. _____. "Computer music: analysis, synthesis, and composition." *Journal of the Acoustical Society of America* 39 (1966), 1245. Abstract.

A description is given of the adaptation of Mathews' MUSIC IV program for use at University of California at Los Angeles. Advantages of higher sample rates, applications of random number techniques, and problems of Fourier synthesis of tones having inharmonic overtones are discussed.

874. _____. "Ethics and esthetics of computer composition." In *The Computer and Music,* ed. Harry B. Lincoln. Ithaca: Cornell University Press, 1970. 37-41.

The author discusses the ultimate human responsibility for ethical and aesthetic judgements in the use of computers in musical composition.

875. _____. "The problem of imperfection in computer music." In *Music by Computers,* ed. H. von Foerster and J.W. Beauchamp. New York: Wiley and Sons, 1969. 133-139.

Emphasis is placed on the importance of irregularities that occur naturally in musical instrument tones and which offer more aesthetic potential than the perfectly periodic waveforms produced by oversimplified acoustic models for synthesis. The author's experiments at UCLA, with a MUSIC IV program, in attempting to introduce irregularity or 'quasi-periodicity' into synthesis programming are presented. Recorded examples are included with the book.

876. Strapac, Susan. "MUSICOMP 76." *Computers and the Humanities* 10, 6 (Nov.-Dec. 1976), 343-344.

Report on a workshop held at State University of New York at Binghamton, July 7-23, 1976, on computers and music.

877. Strasser, Bruce E.; and Max V. Mathews. *Music from Mathematics*. Murray Hill, N.J.: Bell Telephone Laboratories, 1961. 24 pp.

Booklet describing the early research of Max V. Mathews at Bell Telephone Laboratories and his historical antecedents. This was prepared to accompany a 10" disc released later, with compositions by Mathews, Pierce, Guttman, and others.

878. Strawn, John. "Record review-- *Unplayed by Human Hands*." *Computer Music Journal* 1, 3 (June 1977), 53.

Review of a recording entitled *Unplayed by Human Hands*, produced by means of a PDP-8 computer interfaced with a 90-rank, 6-division Schlicker organ at the All Saint's Church in Pasadena, Texas. One composition by V. Ussachevsky, "Fantasy: Everything is Computerized," is included.

879. _____. "Review." *Computer Music Journal* 2, 4 (Dec. 1978), 6-9.

Review of *Kobrin: Computer in Performance* (W. Berlin: Berliner Kuenstlerprogramm des Deutschen Akademischen Austauschdienstes, 1977). See Kobrin.

880. Strong, William; and Melville Clark, Jr. "Perturbations of synthetic orchestral wind instrument tones." *Journal of the Acoustical Society of America* 41, 2 (1967), 277-285.

The relative significance of spectral and
temporal envelopes for the synthesis of
orchestral wind instrument tones through
digital means is evaluated. The simulated
spectral envelopes of the synthesized tones
were systematically 'perturbed' or distorted
so as to determine whether the spectral envelope is vital to recognition of a given
tone quality.

881. _____; _____. "Synthesis of wind
instrument tones." *Journal of the Acoustical*
Society of America 41, 1 (Jan. 1966), 39-52.

Clarinet, oboe, bassoon, tuba, flute, trumpet,
trombone, French horn, and English horn
tones have been synthesized with partials
controlled by one spectral envelope (fixed
for each instrument) and three temporal
envelopes. These tones were tested by a
musically literate audience with fair success.

882. _____. See Plitnik and Strong.

883. Struve, Bill. "A $19 music interface (and some
music theory for computer nuts)." *Byte*
2, 12 (Dec. 1977), 48.

Melody generator to be interfaced with a
small computer is described. Basic music
theory is also included in this article
intended for computer hobbyists.

884. Suchoff, Michael. A microprocessor-based
controller for a live-performance music
synthesizer. Paper presented at the 61st
convention of the Audio Engineering Society,
New York, Nov. 3-6, 1978.

A microprocessor has been used to interface
a keyboard and control panel with analog
sound-generating circuitry, at Arp Instruments. Features include a 16-voice editing
programmer, keyboard tuning of oscillator
parameters, and a real-time 'arpeggiation
sequencer,' incorporated in a polyphonic
synthesizer.

885. Sulitka, Andrej. "K problematike informácií a
základných údajov o ludovej piesni pri
spracování na SP." *Lidová píseň a samočinný
počítač I*, ed. Dušan Holý and Oldřich
Sirovátka. Brno: Klub uživatelů MSP, 1972.
103-110.

886. Summer, R.K.   See Simon and Summer.

887. Sutcliffe, Alan. "Xenakis on computers." *Page:
bulletin of the Computer Arts Society* [U.K.]
34 (Feb. 1975), 2.
Interview with Iannis Xenakis.

888. Svane, Henrik.   See Pedersen and Svane.

889. Sychra, Antonin. "Die Anwendung du Kybernetik
und der Informationstheorie in der marxist-
ischen Ästhetik." *Beiträge zur Musikwissenschaft* 12 (1970), 83-108.

Wide-ranging article dealing with music,
cybernetics, information theory and marxist
political theories. Reference is made to
the work of A.A. Moles and T. Adorno.

890. _____. "Hudba a Kybernetika." *Nové cesty
Hudby* 1 (1964), 234-267. Summary in Ger.
pp. 278-279.

Cybernetics and music are discussed.

891. _____. "Möglichkeiten der Andwendung der
     Kybernetik und der Informationstheorie in
     der marxistischen Musikwissenschaft."
     Beiträge zur Musikwissenschaft 7 (1965),
     402-407.

     Early stages in an attempt to relate music,
     cybernetics, information theory, and marxist
     political thought.

892. "Syncopation by automation." *Data from Electro-
     data*, Aug. 1956, 2-3.

893. Szlifierski, Krzysztof. "Technologie nouvelle
     et initiation des compositeurs à la musique
     expérimentale." *La Revue Musicale* 268-269
     (1971), 149-155.

     Also, as "New technology and the training of
     composers in experimental music." *Music
     and Technology*. Paris: La Revue Musicale,
     1971. 151-156.

     The director of the Experimental Music Studio
     of the Polish Radio in Warsaw expresses his
     views on the technological skills and modern
     musical craftmanship that should be taught
     to young composers, including computer tech-
     niques.

894. Talambiras, R.P. "Digital-to-analog converters:
     some problems in producing high fidelity
     signals." *Computer Design*, Jan. 1967,
     63-69.

     Engineering viewpoint on problems of D/A
     converters in audio applications.

895. _____. Some considerations in the design
     of wide-dynamic-range audio digitizing
     systems. Paper presented to the 57th
     convention of the Audio Engineering
     Society, Los Angeles, May 10-13, 1977.
     Preprint No. 1226.

896. Tamba, Akira. *Sōi to Sōzō*. Diss., Université
     de Paris-- Sorbonne, 1974. 245 pp. Tokyo:
     Ongaku-no tomo, 1972. 326 pp. Summary in
     French.

     A study of twelve contemporary French
     composers, including I. Xenakis and
     P. Barbaud.

897. Tanner, P. MUSICOMP, an experimental aid for
     the composition and production of music.
     ERB-869, National Research Council of
     Canada, Radio and Electrical Engineering
     Division, Ottawa, 1972.

898. Tänzer, Peter. "Der computer als Lektor."
     Musik und Bildung 4, 10 (Oct. 1972),
     461-465.

     Review in *Computers and the Humanities*
     9, 2 (March 1975), 88.

899. _____. "Musik und Kybernetik." *Neue
     Zeitschrift für Musik* 134, 8 (1973),
     483-492.

     Music is portrayed as a cybernetic system.
     The ideas of continuous random movement
     and overall stasis are dealt with and the
     use of the computer to reconcile this
     dichotomy is described. Scores, diagrams
     included.

900. _____; and Erich Neumann. "Computer machen Musik." *Neue Zeitschrift für Musik* 130, 7/8 (1969), 360-362.

A program has been written which specifies chromatic, equal-tempered pitches of two octaves, 4/4 time and rhythmic notation, and a harmonic progression. Within these stipulations the computer 'improvises.'

901. Taylor, G.T. See Powner, Green, and Taylor.

902. Taylor, Hal. "SCORTOS: implementation of a music language." *Byte* 2, 9 (Sept. 1977), 12.

The author's software design is described for use with a music system consisting of an Altair 8800 computer (32K bytes of programmable memory and ROM) with a video terminal or cassette floppy disk and both a mini-Moog electronic sound synthesizer and a Farfisa VIP400 electronic organ. Apparently, the system is intended for control of a number of synthesizers and electronic organs. Music symbols may be typed in at the terminal keyboard.

903. Tempelaars, Stan. "Voltage control in the Utrecht University Studio." *Electronic Music Reports* 1 (Sept. 1969), 61-67.

The electronic music studio at the Institute of Sonology, University of Utrecht, is described in detail, and the use of a computer there is outlined.

904. _____. "The VOSIM signal spectrum."
Interface 6, 2 (Sept. 1977), 81-96.

The VOSIM sound synthesis system is
based on a signal consisting of a series
of $\sin^2$ pulses with a staircase-shaped
envelope. In this article the spectrum
of such a signal is derived.

905. _____. VOSIM sound synthesis. Paper
presented at the First International
Conference on Computer Music, Massachussetts
Institute of Technology, Oct. 28-31, 1976.

A model has been developed at the Institute
of Sonology, Utrecht, by Werner Kaegi and the
author for the description of Indo-European
speech sounds and has been found useful in
producing musical sounds as well. The model
consists of the sum of two series of pulses,
each consisting of the repetition, periodic
or not, of one or more $\sin^2$ pulses. Experiments were conducted with specifically constructed computer-controlled digital
oscillators.

906. _____; and Werner Kaegi. VOSIM-- a new
sound synthesis system. Paper presented
at the 53rd convention of the Audio Engineering Society, Zurich, March 2-5, 1976.

Revised version in *Journal of the Audio
Engineering Society* 26, 6 (June 1978),
418-425.

VOSIM (voice simulation) is a digital
sound synthesis system for production of
linguistic and musical sounds by means of
tone-burst functions with adjustable
pulse-width and cycle duration. A minimum
description for speech synthesis has been

worked out, reducing the amount of input information needed. This description may be applicable to musical sound synthesis as well.

907. _____; and G.M. Koenig. "The computer at the Institute of Sonology, Utrecht." *Interface* 1, 2 (1972), 167-174.

The hardware configuration (which includes a PDP-15/20 computer) and software implemented at the Institute of Sonology is described. The computing system is used for voltage control and for sound synthesis. Various projects at the institute which led to the purchase of the computer are also described.

908. _____; and J. Scherpenisse. "Exponential decay." *Interface* 5, 4 (Dec. 1976), 207-224.

An analog circuit for generating a staircase-shaped envelope for synthesized tones is described. The purpose is to approximate an exponential envelope by means of the staircase function for use in conjunction with the VOSIM experiments in digital sound synthesis. The technique is used to save calculation time in cases where the signal is produced with the aid of a computer and when a constant attenuation per period of a signal is desired.

909. Tenney, James. "Computer music experiments, 1961-1964." *Electronic Music Reports* 1 (Sept. 1969), 22-61.

Excerpted in *Cybernetic Serendipity*, ed. Jasia Reichardt. New York: Praeger, 1969. 21.

Also, in *Musik und Bildung* 3 (1971), 355-358. (Excerpts. See below.)

The author gives a detailed description of his work at Bell Telephone Laboratories, including the compositions *Analog No. 1-- Noise Study, Four Stochastic Studies, Dialogue, Stochastic String Quartet, Ergodos I, Ergodos II, Phases,* and various psychoacoustic experiments. Graphical scores and 'instrument' diagrams included.

910. _____. "Musical composition with the computer." *Journal of the Acoustical Society of America* 39 (1966), 1245. Abstract.

A set of composing problems for use with Mathews' MUSIC IV sound-generation program, specifying time-varying statistical conditions based on stochastic processes and perception of gestalt, are suggested.

911. _____. "Noise study." *Musik und Bildung* 3 (July-Aug. 1971), 355-358.

This essay by the composer describes the processes used in his computer composition *Analog No. 1-- Noise Study.*

912. _____. "The physical correlates of timbre." *Gravesaner Blätter/Gravesano Review* 26 (1965), 103-109.

Natural sounds are taken as a model for the production of rich and varied timbres by means of digital synthesis. Spectrum, transient phenomena, and modulation processes are proposed as the three basic parameters of timbre, and variations in these are perceivable and necessary for

the production of rich timbres. A new definition of timbre is also proposed.

913. _____. "Sound generation by means of a
digital computer." *Journal of Music Theory*
7 (1963), 24-70.

The process of digital synthesis is described
in detail, beginning with definitions of the
various unit generators which are combined
to form 'instruments,' random number generators, conversion function subroutines, and
program language description of 'instruments.'
An example from a score by Tenney, graphs,
and diagrams are included.

914. _____. See Mathews, Miller, Pierce, and
Tenney.

915. Terry, Kenneth. "Charles Dodge: synthesized
speech researcher." *Page: bulletin of the
Computer Arts Society* 41 (Nov. 1978), n.p.

Also, in *downbeat* 45, 1 (Jan. 12, 1978),
23.

Interview with Dodge and brief discussion of
his music. This issue of *Page* also includes
a soundsheet recording of the first part of
Dodge's *In Celebration* (available in its
entirety from Composers' Recordings, Inc.,
CRI348).

916. Tew, M.L. "Interval combinations, predetermined
by the computer, as the harmonic basis of
contemporary music." *The Composer* [U.S.A.]
1 (1969-70), 157-164.

917. Thome, Diane Deutsch. Toward structural
characterization of the timbral domain.
Diss., Princeton University, 1974. 75 pp.
Dissertation Abstracts 34 (Feb. 1974),
5236A-7A.

A new attitude toward waveform transformation, made possible by digital sound synthesis through manipulation of inner partials, is expounded. The author's own composition *Polyvalence* is presented.

918. Tipei, Sever. "MP1: a computer program for
music composition." In *Composition with
Computers*, Proceedings of the Second Annual
Music Computation Conference, Nov. 7-9,
1975, part 2. Urbana: University of
Illinois, 1975. 68-82.

MP1 is a language based on an algorithm
for performing some of the composer's
simpler routine work. The emphasis is on
the processes of probability and chance,
with other features also available. The
output is a string of musical symbols to
be translated for voices or instruments.
A fragment from one of the author's own
compositions is included as an example.

919. Tisato, Graziano. An interactive software
system for real-time sound synthesis.
Paper presented at the First International
Conference on Computer Music, Massachussetts
Institute of Technology, Oct. 28-31, 1976.

A real-time digital sound-synthesis system
designed for the IBM 360/370 computer is
described. The purpose was to provide a
simpler programming language for composers
and researchers, with instant feedback
also available. Samples are generated by

means of Chowning's frequency modulation
technique or other fast algorithms.

920. Tjernlund, Per. "Eine statische Methode für
Grundfrequenzmessungen mit einem Computer."
In *Studia Instrumentorum musicae popularis
II*, ed. Erich Stockmann. Stockholm: Musik-
historiska museet, 1972. 77-81.

Description of the use of digital sound
synthesis in acoustical analysis and
applications of the theory of probability
in music.

921. "Tom Swift and the electronic muse." *High Fidel-
ity/Musical America* 21, 3 (March 1971), 34.

922. Tonietti, Tito. "The computer and music."
Nuova Rivista Musicale Italiana 5 (1971),
1092-1096.

Review of Lincoln's *The Computer and Music*.

923. Torrens, Phillipe. "Avantgard im Framreich."
Melos 40, 6 (1973), 330-338.

A number of younger French composers are
listed here, with short bibliographies and
descriptions of their works, under various
categories; Pierre Barbaud and Iannis Xenakis
are characterized as composers making special
use of mathematics and computers in music.
Also included are Jeanine Charbonnier,
Michel Phillippot, and Jean-Claude Risset.

924. Treble, D.P. "Computers and composition in
change ringing." *Computer Journal* 13, 4
(Nov. 1970), 350-351.

Change ringing is the art of ringing a set of tuned bells in a continually varying order. The author has written several programs that produce blocks of changes of varying length which begin and end with rounds but otherwise contain no repetitions, in Plain Bob Minor. The aim is towards a systematic way of producing compositions for change-ringers. The work of Papworth in 1960 is mentioned.

925. Truax, Barry. "A communicational approach to computer sound programs." *Journal of Music Theory* 20, 2 (Fall 1976).

Excerpts reprinted as "The POD system of interactive composition programs." *Computer Music Journal* 1, 3 (June 1977), 30-39.

The author's POD system of programs for real-time synthesis and interactive composition is described. The basic programs use either fixed waveform synthesis with amplitude modulation or the frequency modulation technique developed by John Chowning. A higher level program calculates non-real-time pressure functions that can be mixed and output at high smapling rates. The compositional structure embodied in the POD programs is examined in detail. An excerpt of the author's work *Trigon* for alto flute, voice, piano, and computer-synthesized tape is included.

926. _____. "The computer composition-- sound synthesis programs POD4, POD5, and POD6." *Sonological Reports* [Utrecht] 2 (1973). 57 pp.

Sound production and compositional organization is realized in real-time with smaller computers (PDP-15) using these programs.

927. _____. "Computer music in Canada." *Numus-West* [Mercer Island, Washington] 2, 2 (Aug. 1975), 17-26.

An overview of types of digital synthesis systems is first given. Detailed description of synthesis systems and information on compositions and activities at the University of Toronto, the Groupe Informatique/Musique in Montreal, the National Research Council in Ottawa, Simon Fraser University, Queen's University, McGill University, and York University is then offered.

928. _____. "General techniques of computer composition programming." *Numus-West* [Mercer Island, Washington] 4 (1973), 17-20.

Voltage control or digital control of digital oscillators is suggested to allow facility in producing multiple events. Several designs of user control, input systems, and a model for generating data arrays are discussed.

929. _____. The inverse relation between generality and strength in computer music programs. Paper presented at the First International Conference on Computer Music, Massachussetts Institute of Technology, Oct. 28-31, 1976.

The range of compositional problems to which a given computer program may be applied vs.

the efficiency of the problem solution is considered. The importance of strong, limited methods for real-time synthesis and compositional systems is emphasized, with examples given from the author's POD system.

930. _____. "Organizational techniques for C:M ratios in frequency modulation." *Computer Music Journal* 1, 4 (Nov. 1977), 39-45.

Useful 'rules of thumb' are given for results obtained when using a given carrier to modulator signal ratio and for constants to be found between various FM spectra which can be used musically. These methods arose from use of the author's POD6 program and include predicting the fundamental or organizing C:M ratios according to spectral identity. Tables for producing tones with just scale intervals or for equal-tempered intervals between the carrier and the fundamental are provided. If one wishes to organize timbres systematically, using the FM technique, one must find some way of organizing the C:M ratios.

931. _____. The POD programs for sound synthesis at Simon Fraser University. Dec. 1974. 23 pp. Mimeo.

932. _____. "Some programs for real-time computer synthesis and composition." *Interface* 2, 2 (Dec. 1973), 159-162.

The resulting programs of the author's compositional work with the PDP-15 computer at the Institute of Sonology, Utrecht, are presented.

933. Ungvari, T. "Tonsaettaren-- en datadirigent."
     Nutida Musik 17, 4 (1973-74), 29-32.

934. Ussachevsky, Vladimir. "Applications of modern
     technology in musicology, music theory, and
     composition in the U.S." *Papers of the
     Yugoslav-American Seminar on Music*, ed.
     Malcom Brown. Bloomington: Indiana University
     Press, 1970. 123-142.

     The application of various technological
     tools, including the computer, to various
     aspects of music, including composition, is
     discussed. A classified bibliography is
     included.

935. Valentin, Karl-Otto. "Om operaarbetet i EMS."
     Nutida Musik 12, 1 (1968-69), 19-20.

     Description of the electronic music studio
     with digital controls in Stockholm.

936. Valinsky, Eric. "Performances at the International
     Computer Music Conference." *Synapse* 2, 4
     (Jan.-Feb. 1978), 12.

     The computer music conference held at the
     University of California, San Diego, Oct.
     26-30, 1977 is reviewed here. The following
     works were mentioned: *Solo for Bass and
     Melody Driven Electronics* by David Behrman,
     using a KIM-1 microprocessor; *Loops for
     Instruments* by Robert Erickson, realized at
     the Stanford Artificial Intelligence Center
     by John Grey; *Percussion Loops* for percussion-
     machine by Robert Erickson; *Plot* for percus-
     sionist by Herbert Brün; *In Deserto* by Jon
     Appleton; *Time into Pieces* by Wesley Fuller;
     Effeti Collaterali by James Dashow; *Traveling
     Music* by Loren Rush; *Inharmonique* by J.-C.
     Risset.

937. Vercoe, Barry. "Computer generated sound programs." *Proceedings of the American Society
of University Composers* 4 (1969), 36-37.

The author discusses his preliminary work
with digital synthesis programs.

938. _____. *Digressions* for voices, instruments
and computer-generated sounds. Diss.,
University of Michigan, 1969. 226 pp.

939. _____. Man-computer interaction as a
creative aid in the formulation of digital
sound structures. Paper presented at the
52nd convention of the Audio Engineering
Society, New York, Oct. 31-Nov. 3, 1975.

Problems inherent in traditional approaches
to composing when using the computer as a
musical instrument are discussed. The
newly-established studio for experimental
music at the Massachussetts Institute of
Technology is described.

940. _____. Man-computer interaction in
creative applications. Cambridge, Studio
for Experimental Music, Nov. 1975.
Unpublished ms.

941. _____. "Music computation conference: a
report and summary." *Perspectives of New
Music* 13, 1 (Fall 1974), 234-238.

This conference on music computation, the
first of its kind, focused on sound synthesis and related research, is reviewed here.
About fifteen papers were presented.

942. _____. "The Music 360 language for sound
synthesis." *Proceedings of the American
Society of University Composers* 6 (1973),
16-20.

The author presents his work in designing
a special acoustical language for encoding
program instructions designated 'instruments'
in a format which facilitates high-speed
digital sound synthesis using the IBM 360
computing system.

943. _____. Reference manual for the Music 360
language for digital sound synthesis. Cambridge,
Studio for Experimental Music, 1973. Mimeo.

Users' manual for Music 360.

944. _____. "Review." *Perspectives of New
Music* 9, 2/10, 1 (Fall-Winter 1971), 323-
330.

Review of H. Lincoln's *The Computer and
Music* and *Musicology and the Computer*, ed.
Barry S. Brook. (New York: City University
of New York Press, 1970. 275 pp.)

945. "Vingt ans de musique." *Revue d'esthetique*
4 (1967), n.p.

946. Wagner, Byron B. Audio snapshots: using an
inexpensive real-time spectrum analyzer
with still-frame and slow-motion capabilities
for electronic music synthesis and speech
recognition. Paper presented to the 60th
convention of the Audio Engineering Society,
Los Angeles, May 2-5, 1978.

A description is given of a microprocessor-
based analyzer which uses a color cathode
ray tube display and stores instantaneous
samples for playback in slow motion. The
intent is the study of sound generation
mechanisms, both electronic and acoustic.
Further applications are also discussed.

947. Warfield, Gerald. Beginner's Manual of
MUSIC 4B. Princeton University Department
of Music, n.d. Mimeo.

Instruction manual on the use of Princeton
University's MUSIC 4B system, developed
from Bell Laboratories' MUSIC IV program.

948. Wedge, Scott. See Rossum and Wedge.

949. Weiland, Frits. "Electronic music in the
Netherlands." *Sonorum Speculum* 33
(Winter 1967-68), 1-20.

Survey of activity in the Netherlands,
centering around the Institute of Sonology
at Utrecht and including the composition
programs with digital synthesis being
developed by G.M. Koenig.

950. _____. "The Institute of Sonology at
Utrecht State University." *Sonorum
Speculum* 52 (1973), 12-27.

Reprinted in *Musical Aspects of the Electronic
Medium*, Report on Electronic Music, ed. F.
Weiland. Utrecht: Institute of Sonology, 1975.

Automated controls for the analog studio and
digital synthesis facilities are described.

951. _____, ed. *Musical Aspects of the Electronic
Medium*, Report on Electronic Music. Utrecht:
Institute of Sonology, 1975. Translated by
Ruth Koenig.

Includes reprints of "Electronic music, 1948-
1953" by L. Cross; "The Institute of Sonology
at Utrecht State University" by F. Weiland;
"The studio at Stockholm" by K. Wiggen; "The
studio in London" by J. Chong; and John
Chowning's "Synthesis of complex audio spectra

by means of frequency modulation." Also
included are lists of studio equipment at
the Urbana, Illinois electronic music studios,
a generalized article by Mathews, Moore, and
Risset at Bell Laboratories, and a short
bibliography.

952. _____. "Relationships between sound and
image." *Electronic Music Reports* 4
(Sept. 1971), 66-91.

Description of experiments and compositions
involving film images and electronic music.
Speculations are made on the sorts of corre-
lations between visual and sonic elements
possible with the use of a computer.

953. *Weltmusiktage Bonn 14.-21. Mai 1977.* Bonn:
Internationale Gesellschaft für Neue Musik,
Section Bundesrepublik Deutschland, 1977.

Biographical information is given on each
of the composers represented at this conference, along with program notes for the compositions presented. Xenakis is included and
describes his current work and procedures in
some detail.

954. Werner, E. See Griese and Werner.

955. Wessel, David L. Low dimensional control of
musical timbre. Paper presented to the 59th
convention of the Audio Engineering Society,
Hamburg, Feb. 28- March 3, 1978. Preprint
No. 1337.

Also, as Centre Georges Pompidou Rapports
IRCAM No. 12, Paris, 1978.

Control schemes for all-digital synthesis
systems employing additive synthesis are

described. These controls are derived from previous perceptual experiments using multi-dimensional scaling techniques. Emphasis is on melodic lines in which timbre is manipulated on a note-to-note basis in the examples. Software for real-time digital sound synthesizers is discussed. A cassette of recorded examples is included with the IRCAM publication.

956. _____. Perceptually based controls for additive synthesis. Paper presented at the First International Conference on Computer Music, Massachussetts Institute of Technology, Oct. 28-31, 1976.

Improvements for additive synthesis systems are suggested, as an outcome of psycho-acoustic research. Timbral dissimilarity is represented as a 'timbre map,' and a regular graded sequence of similar timbres are set up, to be altered systematically. These 'timbre maps' of the alterations are incorporated with an interactive graphic system controlling a digital oscillator bank with small computing system at IRCAM (Institut de Recherche et Coordination Acoustique/Musique).

957. _____. "Psychoacoustics and music: report from Michigan State University." *Page: bulletin of the Computer Arts Society* 30, n.d., n.p.

958. _____; and John Grey. Conceptual structures for the representation of musical material. Centre Georges Pompidou Rapports IRCAM No. 14, Paris, 1978.

A survey of several psychoacoustic experiments using multi-dimensional scaling and

related methods for the representation of
musical material for digital synthesis.

959. _____; and B. Smith. Psychoacoustic aids
for the musician's exploration of new
material. Paper presented at the First
International Conference on Computer Music,
Massachussetts Institute of Technology,
Oct. 28-31, 1976.

960. _____. See Ehresman and Wessel.

961. Westergaard, Peter. "Experimental music."
Journal of Music Theory 3 (1959), 302-306.

Review of Hiller and Isaacson's *Experimental
Music*.

962. White, Gary C. Iowa State Computerized Music
System: MUS, Bulletin No. 1, Ames, Ia.,
April 4, 1973.

Overview is given of a digitally controlled
analog studio under development at Iowa State
University, called ISMUS.

963. _____; Terry A. Smay; and Stefan M.
Silverston. "Iowa State Computer Music
System (ISMUS)." *Page: bulletin of the
Computer Arts Society* 35, n.d., n.p.

The projected system will make use of a
PDP 11-20 computer, Buchla model 218 keyboard, manual controllers, computer periph-.
erals, and an interface with a Buchla
series 200 synthesizer. Hardware and software
design for the system is described.

964. _____. See Silverston and White.

965. Wiggen, Knut. "The electronic music studio at Stockholm: its development and construction." *Interface* 1, 2 (Nov. 1972), 127-165.

Reprinted in *Musical Aspects of the Electronic Medium*, Report on Electronic Music, ed. by F. Weiland. Utrecht: Institute of Sonology, 1971.

The electronic music studio at Stockholm, which includes a PDO 15/40 computer as a control system for other apparatus, is described in detail.

966. _____. "An overview of systems for programming music at the EMS Stockholm." *Page: bulletin of the Computer Arts Society* 32 (1974), n.p.

The hybrid digital-analog studio for electronic music in Stockholm is described.

967. Willson, M. Joseph. A computer-assisted music facility. Paper presented at the 46th convention of the Audio Engineering Society, New York, Sept. 10-13, 1973.

Description is offered of a system that has been assembled at the University of Penn.-Moore School of Engineering: an ARP synthesizer, RMI electric piano/harpsichord, a PDP-8 computer, and a Univac series 70 computer. It is suggested that a new class of hybrid systems is possible.

968. _____. See Smoliar and Willson.

969. Wilson, Sven. "Kan datamaskinen vara tonsättare?" *Nutida Musik* 12, 1 (1968-69), 48-49.

Introduction to the topic of computers being used in music-making.

970. Winckel, Fritz. "Berliner Elektronik."
     Melos 30 (1963), 279-283.

     Trends in electronic music are discussed,
     including Xenakis' idea of stochastic music
     and recent attempts to apply information
     theory to music.

971. _____, ed. *Experimentelle Musik. Raum-*
     Musik, Medien Musik, Wort Musik, Elektronik
     Musik, Computer Musik. Internationale Woche
     für experimentelle Musik 1968. Schriftenreihe
     der Akademie der Künste Berlin 7. Berlin:
     Gebrüder Mann, 1970. 101 pp.

     Includes an article by Heinz Zemanek, "Aspekte
     der Informationsverarbeitung und Computer-
     anwendung in der Musik." See Zemanek.

972. Winham, Godfrey. "How MUSIC 4B generates formants
     and non-harmonic partials, and improves
     loudness control and 'quality.'" *Proceedings*
     of the American Society of University Compos-
     ers 1 (1968), 42-46.

     Description of the central features of
     Princeton University's MUSIC 4B system,
     which make it possible to synthesize non-
     harmonic spectra, variable amplitudes for
     different partials, and spectral envelopes
     (i.e. 'formants'), to eliminate problems of
     'foldover' of high harmonics of high pitches,
     and to provide an operation which adapts
     amplitude specifications to a response curve
     similar to the Fletcher-Munson curve.

973. _____. The reference manual of MUSIC 4B.
     Princeton University Music Department, 1966.
     Mimeo. 74 pp.

974. _____; and K. Steiglitz. "Input generators
for digital sound synthesis." *Journal of
the Acoustical Society of America* 47, 2-
part 2 (1970), 665-666.

A fast method for generating a periodic
discrete-time signal with harmonics of
equal amplitude and a fundamental frequency
which is not necessarily an integral
fraction of the sampling frequency (as
with ordinary pulse generators). Such a
signal can be used as input to digital
filters for synthesis of speech and music.

975. Wolff, Anthony B. "Problems of representation
in musical computing." *Computers and the
Humanities* 11, 1 (Jan.-Feb. 1977), 3-12.

Discussion of design requirements for
encoding musical notation for printing
processes and also for analytical, compositional, and bibliographical purposes. These
are related to the features of DARMS. The
conclusion is that DARMS is the most comprehensive and well thought-out digital
code representation of musical scores.

976. Wolterink, Charles D. "Stanford University:
The Center for Computer Research in Music
and Acoustics." *Current Musicology* 21
(1976), 7-8.

Description of facilities now possible with
the aid of several grants at Stanford University. The staff is named and objectives
outlined.

977. Wood, Thomas. A high-speed digital-to-analog
conversion system for digital music synthesis.
Paper presented to the 54th convention of
the Audio Engineering Society, Los Angeles,
May 4-7, 1976. Preprint No. 1121.

Review of the specifications necessary to
provide acceptable digital-to-analog conversion for music is given. A system with
a 100K sampling rate and 16-bit resolution,
at the Indiana University School of Music,
is described.

978. Woodbury, Arthur. "*Velox.*" *Source: Magazine of
the Avant-Garde* 4, 1-2 (Jan. 1970), 61.

Sound material produced by the PDP-10 at the
Stanford Artificial Intelligence Project is
subjected to tape manipulations to produce
this composition. A recording is included.

979. Woodward, P.M. "The synthesis of music and
speech." *Computer Journal* 9 (1966-67),
257-262.

A fast general-purpose computer is programmed
purposely to produce machine noises which are
amplified directly and heard through a monitor
loudspeaker. It is possible, through time-
multiplexing, to produce several frequencies
simultaneously, and the author suggests that
the method may be considered seriously for
synthesis of speech or music. The computer
used for these experiments was a RREAC (made
by R.R.E., in Worcester, Eng.)

980. Wörner, Karl H. *History of Music*. Translated and supplemented by Willis Wager. New York: Free Press, 1973. 712 pp.

The principal developments in West European music from pre-historic times to the 1970's is presented, with the role played by technology in modern music-making included in the final pages.

981. Xenakis, Iannis. "Auf der Suche nach einer stochastischen Musik"/"In search of a stochastic music." *Gravesaner Blätter* 4, 11-12 (1958), 98-122.

982. _____. Formilisation et axiomatisation de la composition musicale. Paper presented in Berlin, 1964.

Also, in *Musique. Architecture*, collection of Xenakis' papers. Tournai: Casterman, 1971. 20-25.

983. _____. "Free stochastic music from the computer." In *Cybernetics, the Arts, and Ideas*, ed. Jasia Reichardt. Greenwich, Ct.: New York Graphic Society, 1971. 124-142.

Also, appears in French as chapter 4 of Xenakis' *Musiques Formelles*. Paris: Editions Richard-Masse, 1971.

A different English translation appears in *Formalized Music*, by Xenakis. Bloomington: Indiana University Press, 1971.

Also, in Ger. and Eng. in *Gravesaner Blätter* 7, 26 (1965), 54-92. This issue includes a supplemental phonodisc, with the Bernade String Quartet playing the work *ST/4-1,080262*. The recording was produced at the Gravesano Experimental-studio Hermann Scherchen.

The composer's concept of 'stochastic music' is explained and the composition program used by him to produce a work for string quartet is presented. This was accomplished at the Paris Institut Européen de Calcul Scientifique, Compaignie IBM France, using an IBM 7090 computer.

984. _____. "Grundlagen einer stochastischen Musik"/"Elements of a stochastic music." *Gravesaner Blätter* 5, 18 (1960), 61-105; 5, 19-20 (1960), 128-150; 6, 21 (1961), 102-121; 6, 22 (1961), 131-155.

Exposition on the composer's work with computer programming to produce a music bounded by laws of probability or other mathematical formulae.

985. _____. *Musique. Architecture.* Collection 'Mutations-Orientations' No. 11. Tournai: Casterman, 1971. 160 pp.

Collection of essays, papers given at conferences, radio broadcast programs, etc., by Xenakis. Included are: "Théorie des probabilités et composition musicale," "Les trois paraboles," "Formilisation et axiomatisation de la composition musicale," "Trois poles de condensation," "Vers une metamusique," "Vers une philosophie de la musique," and several papers on architecture. The relationship between music and architecture drawn by the composer is made clear here, and his musical philosophy is set forth. See individual articles also.

986. _____. "Musiques Formelles: nouveaux principes formels de composition musicales." *La Revue Musicale* 253-254 (1963), entire issue.

Also, as *Musiques Formelles*. Paris: Editions Richard-Masse, 1963. 232 pp.

Also, as *Formalized Music*, translated by C.A. Butchers, G.W. Hopkins, J. Challifour, and A. Challifour. Bloomington: Indiana University Press, 1971. 271 pp.

Detailed analyses of Xenakis' own work and descriptions of his compositional processes are presented. The composer's philosophical basis for his use of the computer is expounded. Diagrams, flow-charts, tables, and the complete printout of his program, Free Stochastic Music, in FORTRAN, are included. Details of mathematical formulae translated into musical experience, data for the work *Atrees*, and several bars of musical transcription of *ST/10-1,080262* are also included. The final chapter proposes a theory of 'microsound structure' as a basis for further compositions using computer-generated sound.

987. _____. "Théorie des probabilités et composition musicale." In *Musique. Architecture*. Tournai: Casterman, 1971. 1-16.

Also, as "Wahrscheinlichkeitstheorie und musik." *Gravesaner Blätter/Gravesano Review* 1, 6 (1956), 28-34.

The composer discusses his use of probability theory, regarded by him as a mirror of natural and modern-day social phenomena to be translated into works of art.

988. _____. "Les trois paraboles." *Nutida Musik* 4 (1958), n.p.

Also, in *Musique. Architecture.* Tournai: Casterman, 1971. 16-19.

The geometry of the 1958 Philips Pavilion in Brussels, designed by Le Corbusier with Xenakis assisting, is applied to musical composition here by Xenakis.

989. _____. "Trois poles de condensation." Broadcast program, Radio Varsovie, 1962.

Also, in *Musique. Architecture.* Tournai: Casterman, 1971. 26-37.

990. _____. "Vers une métamusique." *La Nef* 29 (1967), n.p.

Reprinted in *Musique. Architecture.* Tournai: Casterman, 1971. 38-70.

Also, as "Towards a metamusic." In *Cybernetics, the Arts, and Ideas,* ed. Jasia Reichardt. Greenwich, Ct.: New York Graphic Society, 1971. 111-123.

A different Eng. translation also appears in *Formalized Music,* by Xenakis. Bloomington: Indiana University Press, 1971.

991. _____. "Vers une philosophie de la musique." *Gravesaner Blätter* 8, 29 (1966), 88-114.

Also, in *Revue d'Esthetique* [Paris] 2-3-4 (1968), 173-210.

Also, in *Musique. Architecture.* Tournai: Casterman, 1971. 71-119.

992. "Xenakis." *L'Arc* 51 (1972), 88.

An interview with the composer is presented,
along with essays on his music by Bernard
Pingaud, Daniel Durney, Oliver Revault
D'Allones, Maurice Fleuret, François Genuys,
François Bernard Mâche, and Hanspeter
Krellman. Also included are two essays on
his architectural works and studies of the
compositions *Pithoprakta* and *Polytope*.

993. "Xenakis." *La Revue Musicale* 265-266 (1969),
43-50.

Notes on compositions performed at a festival
of Xenakis' music, Oct. 26, 1969, at the
Musée d'Art Moderne de la Ville de Paris.

994. "Iannis Xenakis parle." Disque de la collection
d'Homme d'Aujourd'hui, no. 55. Realisation
sonore Hugues Desalle, 4, Villa du Pont-de-
Grenelle, Paris, 15e.

995. Yates, Peter. "Musical computers at Urbana."
Arts and Architecture 82, 6 (June 1965),
8, 34-35.

Description of early work with sound
generation at University of Illinois,
Champaign-Urbana.

996. _____. *Twentieth Century Music*. New York:
Pantheon Books, 1967.

General textbook on modern music, which
includes some mention of the use of computers in music and provides the background against which these developments
took place.

997. Young, Frederick J. "Open tones of musical horns." *Journal of the Acoustical Society of America* 40 (1966), 1252. Abstract.

998. Youngblood, Joseph E. "Letter to the editor." *Computers and the Humanities* 7 (1972-73), 28.

A letter referring to Mathews' *Technology of Computer Music*.

999. Zaripov, Rudolf Khafizovich. *Kibernetika i muzyka*. Moscow: Znanie, 1963.

English trans. by J.G.K. Russell in *Perspective of New Music* 7, 2 (Spring-Summer 1969), 115-154.

This is the only Soviet book to date on the applications of computers to musical data processing. It deals mainly with computational musicology and composition according to known styles of existing works, rather than original works, but the author does speculate on other possiblities. Additional commentary by Michael Kassler.

1000. _____. *Kibernetika i muzyka*. Moscow: Nauka, 1971. 235 pp.

English abstract in *Soviet Cybernetics Review* 1, 6 (Nov. 1971), 64.

This monograph examines cybernetics as it relates to the activity of a composer. Prehistory is given, followed by a survey of Soviet and other work done with composing and analyzing music with the aid of computers. Projects on the synthesis of sound for acoustical and psychophysiological investigations are described. Also presented is a program which produces melodies, songs, and harmonization, and a prototype of a teaching system.

1001. _____. "O Programirovanyii Processza Szocsinyija." *Problemy Kibernetyiki* 7 (1962), 151-160.

1002. _____. "On an algorithmic description of the process involved in the composition of music (ARTINT)." *Automation Express* 3, 3 (Nov. 1960), 17-19.

Russian version in *Doklady Akademiia Nauk SSR* 132 (1960), 1283-1286.

A description is given of an algorithm simulating a compositional process for an instrumental solo piece. The compositional rules and the logic of the program are explained and a sample of a piece produced this way is included.

1003. Zemanek, Heinz H. "Aspekte der Informationsverarbeitung und Computeranwendung in der Musik." in *Experimentelle Musik,* ed. Fritz Winckel. Berlin: Mann, 1970. 59-72.

The author investigates the potential for the use of the computer in the arts, especially in music, from the standpoint of its abilities to store data, to perform routine work, and to recognize and follow rules. An ideal is projected of the composer working at a computer console with complete intuitive concentration.

1004. _____. "Automaten und Denkprozesse." In
Digital Information Processors, ed. Walter
Hoffman. New York: Interscience, 1962.
1-66.

1005. Zieliński, Gerard. "Komputerowa simulacja
komponowania muzyki." *Prace centrum
obliczeniowego, PAN 19*. Warsaw: Cenztrum
Obliczeniowe Polskiej Akademii Nauk, 1970.
18 pp. Mimeo. In Pl., with summaries in
Eng., Ru.

Preliminary considerations concerning the
mathematical description of musical ideas
are first outlined. The author then presents
his own work which uses a mathematical model
for simulation of the compositional process.

1006. _____. "Zastowania komputerow w sztuce."
Prace centrum obliczeniowego, PAN 81. Warsaw:
Centrum Obliczeniowe Polskiej Akademii Nauk,
1972. 16 pp. Mimeo. In Pl., with summaries
in Eng., Ru.

Computer applications in the arts, particularly in music, are discussed. Polish experiments are described.

1007. Ziljstra, M. "Computer-poezie." *Mens en Mel*
29 (April 1974), 120-122.

1008. _____. "Het componeren van de avant-garde
in de 20ste eeuw." *Mens en Mel* 31 (Jan.
1976), 3.

Xenakis is the subject of this article.

1009. Zilynskyj, Orest. "Text lidové písně jako
předmět strojového rozboru." *Lidová píseň
a samocinný počítač I*, ed. Dušan Holý and
Oldřich Sirovátka. Brno: Klub uživatelů MSP,
1972. 97-102. Summary in Eng.

1010. Zimmerman, Franklin B. "Computer music." *Computers and the Humanities* 6 (1971-72), 293-294.

Review of Mathews' *The Technology of Computer Music*.

1011. Zimmerman, Walter. *Desert Plants-* Conversations with 25 American Composers. Vancouver, B.C.: Walter Zimmerman and ARC Publications, 1978.

1012. Zingheim, T. Joseph. "Introduction to computer music techniques." *Electronotes* 6, 42 (Aug. 5, 1974), 1-5.

Introductory article describing both sound generation and analog control by means of computers, in engineering terms.

1013. Zinovieff, Peter. "A computerized electronic music studio." *Electronic Music Reports* 1 (Sept. 1969), 5-22.

A description is given of a computer installation including an 8K PDP8/S and a 4K PDP8/L computer, with interface and sound-producing peripherals and both digitally and voltage-controlled equipment. Diagrams of hardware configuration of the Putney (London) studio and a brief description of the programming are included.

1014. _____. "Two electronic music computer projects in Britain." In *Cybernetic Serendipity*, ed. Jasia Reichardt. New York: Praeger, 1969; London: McKay, 1968. 28-29.

Description of automated features in the hybrid digital-analog systems at the London electronic music studio developed by the author.

1015. _____. VOCOM: a synthetical engine. London, Technical Report of the Electronic Music Studio London, Ltd., 1972.

Technical report on the author's studio describing a system including a PDP8/S and a PDP/L with interface to analog hardware.

1016. Zuckerman, Mark; and Kenneth Steiglitz. "Using circulant Markov chains to generate waveforms for music." *Software Synthesis Techniques*, Proceedings of the Second Annual Music Computation Conference, Nov. 7-9, 1975, part 1. Urbana: University of Illinois, 1975. 58-76.

A unique method for generating complex sound spectra has been developed at the Godfrey Winham Laboratory at Princeton University, using circulant Markov chains. These are used in this application entirely for sound generation rather than compositional processes. The result is similar to that of recursive digital filtering. With the appropriate modifications, a variety of characteristics may be attained.

1017. _____. See Cann, Lansky, Steiglitz, and Zukerman.

List of Computer Acronyms in Common Use

A/D and D/A conversion: analog-to-digital and digital-to-analog conversion

CPU: central processing unit

CRT: cathode ray tube

ECL: emitter-coupled logic

IC: integrated circuit

LSI: large scale integrated circuit

RAM: random access memory

ROM: read only memory

TTL: transistor-transistor logic

Some Manufacturers of Computers and Computer Components
with a partial listing of their products

company, address	models, products
Adage, Inc. Boston, Mass. Now defunct.	Ambilog (30 bits, a hybrid digital-analog computer).
American Microsystems, Inc. 3800 Homestead Rd. Santa Clara, Cal. 95051	integrated circuits, peripherals-- AMI6800 intelligent terminal.
Apple Computer, Inc. 10260 Bandley Dr. Cupertino, Cal. 95014	Apple I and Apple II, microcomputers.
Applied Microtechnology 100 N. Winchester Blvd. Suite 260 Santa Clara, Cal. 95050	AMT 2650, microprocessor.
Barr and Stroud, Ltd. United Kingdom	SOLIDAC (early model using vacuum tubes).
Burroughs Corporation Burroughs Plaza Detroit, Michigan 48232	5000, 5500, 6500, 6700, other models large computers. 1700 (16 bits). peripherals.
Computer Automation, Inc. 2181 Dupont Dr. Irvine, Cal. 42713	LSI-2, LSI-4, Naked/Mini LSI.

company, address	products
Control Data Corporation 8100 34th Ave., S. Minneapolis, Minn. 55440	CDC 6600 (60 bits), CDC 6400, 6800, and other large systems. (The 6400 was used by the PLATO system.) CYBER series. peripherals, including intelligent terminals.
Data General Corporation Rte. 9 Westbo, Mass. 01581	Nova (16 bits) and variants: Supernova, Nova 1200, and Nova 800. MicroNova.
Digital Computer Controls, Inc. 12 Industrial Rd. Fairfield, N.J. 07006	DCC-116 (16 bits); DCC-112 (12 bits).
Digital Equipment Corp. (DEC) 146 Main St. Maynard, Mass. 01754	PDP-1, PDP-4, PDP-9, PDP-15 (all 18 bits); PDP-6 (36 bits); PDP-12 (12 bits); PDP-8 series, LINC-8 (12 bits); PDP-10 (formerly PDP-6, also called DECsystem-10, 36 bits); LSI-11 micro- processor; PDP-11 (16 bits); peripherals.
Digital Scientific Corp. 11455 Sorrento Valley Rd. San Diego, Cal. 92121	META 4 (16 bits).

company, address	products
Fairchild Microsystems Div. 1725 Technology Drive San Jose, Cal. 95110	9440 (16 bits), MiniFormulator.
General Electric Business Division 401 North Washington St. Rockville, Md. 20850	GEPAC 4010, GEPAC 4020; Mark I, II, III (far-reaching time- sharing systems).
General Instrument Corp. 1775 Broadway New York, N.Y. 10019	CP-1600 .
GRI Computer Corp. 320 Needham St. Newton, Mass. 02164	GRI-99 (16 bits) and other minicomputer models.
Heath Company Benton Harbor, Mich. 49022	H-11 (16 bits) com- puter kit, using LSI-11 microprocessor from DEC; H-8 kit, using 8080A micro- processor; peripherals.
Hewlitt-Packard Corp. 1501 Page Mill Rd. Palo Alto, Cal. 94394	HP 2100 series (16 bits) and various other large machines; HP 9831A desk-top computer; peripherals.
Honeywell Corp. Honeywell Plaza Minneapolis, Minn. 55408	H-316 (16 bits); DDP-516 (16 bits); DDP-716 (16 bits).

company, address	products
IMS Associates, Inc. 1922 Republic Ave. San Leandro, Cal. 94577	IMSAI 8080, 8084 (microprocessors); PCS-80; VDP-80; peripherals.
Intel Corporation 3065 Bowers Ave. Santa Clara, Cal. 95051	Intel 8080, 8088 (8 bit microprocessors); 4004 (4 bits), 8086 (16 bits); micro- computer systems; peripherals.
Intelligent Systems Corp. 5965 Peachtree Corners East Norcross, Ga. 30071	microcomputer systems, peripherals.
Interdata, Inc. 2 Crescent Place Oceanport, N.J. 07757	Model 70 and other minicomputers.
International Business Machines (IBM) Old Orchard Rd. Armonk, N.Y. 10504	650 and 700 series (these used vacuum tubes); IBM 7090 and 7094 (36 bits); IBM 360, 370 series; 1130 series (16 bits); IBM 1800 (16 bits); System 7 (16 bits) and System 3 (variable); peripherals.
Lincoln Laboratories P.O. Box 1139 Laboratory Park Decatur, Ill. 62525	LINC (12 bits)-- not sold commercially, but designed for biomedical research and used in various laboratories.

company, address	products
Lockheed Electronics Co., Inc. Data Products Division 6201 East Randolph St. Los Angeles, Cal. 90040	MAC 16 (16 bits); SUE (36, 16 bits).
Martin Research 336 Commercial Ave. Northbrook, Ill. 60062	MIKE III (minicomputer using Intel 8080 micro- processor); MIKE-8 Model 882 (using Z-80 microprocessor).
MITS, Inc. 2450 Alamo S.E. Albuquerque, New Mexico 87106 (Micro Instrumentation and Telemetry Systems, Inc.)	ALTAIR 6800B and ALTAIR 8800B micro- processors; MITS 88- ADC analog-to-digital converter; peripherals.
Modular Computer Systems 2709 North Dixie Highway Ft. Lauderdale, Fla. 33308	MODCOMP series (16 bit minicomputers).
MOS Technology, Inc. 950 Rittenhouse Rd. Norristown, Penn. 19401	MOSTEK microprocessors; KIM-1 microcomputer (uses MOSTEK 6502 microprocessor).
Motorola, Inc. 1303 E. Algonquin Rd. Schaumburg, Ill. 60196	Motorola 6800 micro- processor (8 bits); also, 6800 (16 bits).
National Semiconductor Corp. 2900 Semiconductor Dr. Santa Clara, Cal. 95015	IMP-16C, IMP-16L, 8900, and PACE (all microprocessors); peripherals.

company, address	products
Raytheon, Inc. 141 Spring St. Lexington, Mass. 02173	704, 706, 707 (all early computers).
Sperry-Rand Corporation 1) Sperry Univac Division P.O. Box 500 Blue Bell, Penn. 19422 2) Sperry-Univac Mini-Computer Operations 2722 Michelson Dr. Irvine, Cal. 92664	UNIVAC I (Universal Automatic Computer), first commercial stored-program computer; UNIVAC 1106, 1108, (36 bits); A/D interfaces; peripherals.
Standard Logic, Inc. 2215 S. Standard Ave. Santa Ana, Cal. 92707	CASH-8 (16 bits).
Systems Engineering Laboratories 6901 W. Sunrise Blvd. Ft. Lauderdale, Fla. 33313	810, Systems 72 (16 bits), and other minicomputers.
Tandy Corporation-- Radio Shack 1800 One Tandy Center Fort Worth, Texas 76102	TRS-80 microcomputer (using Z-80 microprocessor).
Texas Instruments, Inc. P.O. Box 225474 Dallas, Texas 75265	TI 960, 960A, 980, 9900 (all 16 bits) microprocessors; peripherals.
University of Illinois Champaign-Urbana, Ill. 61801 (in cooperation with the Burroughs Corp. at earlier stages)	ILLIAC I, II, III, IV (all very large computing systems).

251

company, address	products
Varian Data Machines 2722 Michelson Dr. Irvine, Cal. 92664	Varian 620, 520 (16 bits) and Varian 73, all mini-computers.
Westinghouse Electric Corp. Gateway Center Westinghouse Building Pittsburgh, Penn. 15222	W2500.
Xerox Data Systems, Inc. Los Angeles, Cal. Now defunct.	Sigma 2 (16 bits), Sigma 7, and other large computers.

Index

254

analysis/synthesis of musical instrument tones.
13, 31, 73, 74, 82, 96, 111, 112, 169, 172,
174, 247, 249, 264, 265, 266, 268, 272, 277,
278, 280, 292, 294, 300, 301, 303, 315, 319,
356, 374, 388, 389, 397, 421, 506, 526, 527,
542, 564, 565, 624, 635, 636, 637, 638, 676,
702, 737, 738, 739, 740, 741, 742, 746, 749,
750, 786, 805, 880, 881, 920, 997, 1000.

artificial intelligence and music.
380, 384, 385, 485, 487, 490, 496, 497, 498,
499, 500, 604, 606, 644, 664, 669, 755, 798,
821, 999, 1000, 1001, 1002, 1005.

bibliographies.
19-24, 49, 67, 99, 107, 135, 136, 142, 189,
202, 272, 294, 379, 400, 401, 473, 518, 603,
614, 736, 742, 768, 923, 934.

change-ringing.
668, 924.

compositions, discussions of; excerpts of; reproductions
of.
32, 37, 42, 44, 46, 95, 107, 122, 123, 125,
128, 147, 230, 231, 232, 268, 290, 365, 367,
370, 371, 373, 375, 378, 379, 384, 385, 386,
396, 398, 404, 412, 456, 458, 548, 577, 581,
677, 728, 762, 764, 830, 909, 911, 913, 915,
917, 918, 925, 938, 978, 986, 987, 988, 990,
992, 993.

composition programs.
44, 50, 51, 131, 132, 137, 138, 148, 152,
155, 247, 249, 272, 289, 291, 312, 335, 357,
365-371, 372, 375-379, 380, 381, 384, 385,
386, 387, 461, 462, 463, 464, 465, 466, 467,
468, 469, 470, 478, 479, 480, 481, 482, 490,
497, 512, 513, 516, 542, 550, 581, 583, 588,
599, 612, 617, 621, 640, 641, 644, 653, 664,
714, 715, 716, 719, 720, 721, 722, 755, 756,

845–849, 850, 851, 852, 853, 854, 855, 897,
900, 916, 918, 925, 926, 928, 929, 931, 932,
949, 951, 981, 982, 983, 984, 985, 986, 987,
988, 989, 990, 999, 1002, 1005, 1006.

computers, specific models. (For further information,
see manufacturers list.)
Altair 680: 210.
Altair 8800: 902.
Ambilog 200: 532.
ASI 210: 180, 761.
Burroughs 5500: 532.
Burroughs 6700: 756.
CDC 1604: 74.
CDC 3600: 268, 458, 762.
CDC 6400: 117, 287.
CDC 6600: 190.
CDC 7600: 337.
CSX-1: 74, 79, 229, 378, 381, 383, 515.
DDP-224: 567.
Electrologica X8: 469.
IBM 360/370: 201, 242, 312, 313, 843, 919,
943.
IBM 1620: 665.
IBM 7090: 50ff., 79, 312, 370, 375, 378,
381, 387, 469, 561, 829, 983.
IBM 7094: 74, 123, 128, 300, 371, 454, 554,
561, 665, 725.
ICL 1709: 337.
ICL 1905E: 41.
ICL 2970: 337.
ILLIAC II: 74, 82, 83, 84, 277, 278, 280,
314, 315, 358, 359, 361, 363, 364, 365,
366, 367, 368, 369, 370, 372, 376, 377,
379, 380, 381, 384, 385, 386, 588, 659,
660, 661, 662, 995, 996.
Interdata minicomputer: 209.
KIM-1: 95, 103.
LSI-11: 8ff., 18, 70, 503, 528, 770.
MOS Technology 6502: 175, 656, 657.

Motorola 6800:   341.
Packard-Bell 250:   554.
PDP 5:   425ff.
PDP 9:   344.
PDP 10:   42, 528, 638, 791, 857, 978.
PDP 11:   3, 8, 44ff., 310, 422, 699, 782,
    819, 857, 962, 963, 1013ff.
PDP 15:   847, 907, 925, 926, 930, 932, 949ff.,
    965, 966.
Pegasus: 288.
RREAC: 979.
SC/MP: 587.
SEL 840A: 716.
SOLIDAC: 647.
TI 960A: 117, 330, 539ff.
TI 980A: 89, 90.
Univac 70:   967.
VACuuM: 701, 857.
Xerox Sigma 5: 144.
Xerox Sigma 7: 396, 401, 404, 407, 408.
Xerox Sigma 9:   641.
Zilog Z-80:   654.

conferences and exhibits, reports on.
    85-88, 113, 192, 194, 200, 235, 340, 405,
    448, 517, 542, 667, 713, 759, 760, 818, 867,
    976, 936, 941, 953, 971.

converters, A/D and D/A.
    74, 83, 84, 104, 348, 350-353, 447, 476,
    477, 563, 659, 784, 861, 868, 894.

correlation of sound and image via computers.
    152, 207, 210, 236, 288, 415, 594, 669, 699,
    764, 782, 952.

cybernetics and music. See information processing.

DAC (digital-to-analog converter). See converters,
    D/A and A/D.

digital delay lines.
    198, 354.

digital recording.
    324, 627, 784, 895.

discographies.
    107, 518, 580, 603, 736, 742, 768.

filters, digital.
    8, 82, 94, 422, 433, 434, 435, 436, 505,
    509, 579, 614, 629, 661, 679, 702, 799,
    974, 1016.

fold-over.
    563, 972.

Fourier synthesis; Fourier theorem.
    72, 73, 74, 75, 79, 140, 142, 153, 503, 509,
    614, 630, 799, 972, 974, 1016.

frequency modulation. see modulation, frequency.

graphic art/musical scores as graphic art.
    123, 128, 275.

graphic score-drawing program.
    156, 157, 557.

graphical data input; interactive graphics terminal,
    use of.
    201, 553, 572, 775, 956.

group theory and music.
    59, 61, 181, 665, 986, 992.

histories, chronological surveys.
    36, 47, 135, 154, 162, 203, 247, 267, 275,
    325, 361, 366, 372, 381, 423, 439, 446,
    465, 482, 516, 518, 650, 671, 682, 683,
    684, 687, 709, 712, 951, 970, 980, 996, 1000.

I Ching.
>44, 360, 371, 454.

information processing and music; cybernetics and
>music.
>53, 65, 87, 209, 485, 486, 488, 489, 491,
>492, 493, 494, 495, 512, 821, 975, 1000.

information theory and music.
>189, 334, 339, 364, 365, 380, 384, 385,
>386, 440, 448, 603, 604, 605, 607, 664,
>686, 690, 698, 889, 890, 891, 970, 971,
>999, 1000, 1001, 1003, 1004.

introductions to computer music.
>4, 5, 6, 19, 29, 30, 36, 37, 47, 55, 71,
>105, 135, 143, 154, 159, 204, 233, 262, 263,
>275, 311, 318, 347, 348, 349, 350, 351-354,
>361, 363, 367, 368, 377, 396, 401, 402, 431,
>468, 480, 518, 531, 570, 578, 615, 621, 652,
>656, 857, 872, 892, 969, 1012.

journals, bulletins.
>2, 193, 253, 317, 673, 674, 758.

keyboard instruments.
>9, 10, 11, 17, 18, 35, 133, 134, 178, 220,
>237, 261, 282, 283, 331, 430, 452, 587, 655,
>778, 836, 878, 884, 902, 967.

languages, used in music programs.
>ALGOL: 458, 469, 532.
>APL: 641.
>FORTRAN: 101, 312, 406, 426, 469, 516, 665,
>761, 762, 763.
>LISP: 849.
>machine languages: 201,371, 847, 937, 939,
>942, 943.
>PASCAL: 117.
>SNOBOL: 273.
>special purpose:

C: 3.
DARMS: 245, 246, 247, 250, 713, 975.
Dartmouth system language: 27.
EMS-1: 417.
EUTERPE/EUTERPE2: 845, 847, 848, 851, 854, 855.
EUTERPE-LISP: 849.
GRIN94: 775.
IML: 413.
MP-1: 918.
MUS10: 621.
MUSIC-11: 860.
Musica: 704, 705.
MUSICOL: 577.
MUSICOMP: 268, 356, 370, 375, 387, 512.
NOTRAN: 154.
SCORE: 839, 840, 841.
SCORTOS: 902.
Smalltalk: 443.
SOUND: 190, 191.
SPIRAL: 16.
SYN4B (for Alles-DiGiugno synthesizer): 70, 770.
SYNTAL: 828.
TEMPO: 185, 186.
other: 444, 779, 780, 781, 919.

linear prediction techniques.
145, 447, 629, 630, 679ff.

localization of sound, study and manipulation.
100, 170, 238, 255, 858.

Markov analysis and music; Markov chains in music.
118, 132, 189, 257, 334, 358, 1016.

mathematical functions for sound synthesis.
discrete Hilbert Transform: 432.
Fast Fourier Transform: 432.
Walsh functions: 483, 505.
see also: mathematics and music.

mathematics and music.
57, 58, 59, 60 61, 62, 181, 252, 266, 649, 723, 923, 1005.
see also: algorithms in music; group theory and music; Markov analysis and music; random probability processes, etc.; and serial operations.

melody generators.
63, 118, 132, 207, 515, 622, 698, 715, 716, 720, 722, 846, 859, 883, 995, 1000.

minicomputers, microcomputers, microprocessors.
7, 8, 9, 10, 11, 13, 89, 90, 95, 103, 117, 131, 152, 154, 175, 178, 180, 194, 197, 198, 209, 210, 219, 220, 236, 237, 283, 310, 333, 341, 342, 355, 400, 503, 509, 528, 540, 587, 611, 654, 656, 657, 674, 701, 710, 770, 775, 777, 778, 795, 802, 816, 828, 836, 857, 883, 884, 902, 936, 946, 962, 963.

mixed media, programmed control of.
42, 209, 236, 260, 288, 290, 415, 582, 658, 669, 699, 764, 771, 772, 773.

modulation, amplitude.
31, 101, 170, 218, 299, 541, 858.

modulation, frequency.
137, 140, 142, 172, 443, 508, 509, 536, 641, 795, 796, 805, 856, 858, 919.

musique concrète.
13, 36, 49, 167, 203, 325, 420, 423, 599, 603, 605, 607, 797, 798.

non-linear synthesis techniques.
31, 137, 140, 142, 443, 483, 505, 508, 509, 536, 627, 628, 641, 795, 796, 805, 856, 858, 919.

organs, use of computers with electric and pipe.
35, 144, 216, 430, 452, 878, 902.

overtones, manipulation of.
153, 665, 691, 832, 880, 881, 917, 972.

pedagogy.
14, 15, 35, 45, 91, 92, 93, 176, 182, 185,
259, 323, 356, 464, 466, 497, 499, 620, 641,
819, 893, 1000.

perception, studies of; psychoacoustics.
96, 169, 240, 255, 267, 280, 294, 302, 303,
428, 444, 570, 623, 645, 690, 726, 737, 738,
741, 742, 743, 744, 746, 748, 750, 774, 781,
955, 956, 957, 958, 959, 1000, 1001.

performances, documented or reviewed.
103, 210, 371, 455, 789, 867, 936, 993.

polyphonic synthesizers, with programming capability.
178, 220, 261, 587, 655, 778, 836, 884.

probability, use in music. See random, etc.

programmed control of analog synthesizers, or other
analog sound generators.
general discussion: 38, 39, 86, 203, 204,
239, 276, 374, 377, 518, 521, 608, 609, 610,
615, 651, 654, 777, 802, 844.
specific systems:
ARP Instruments/David Friend: 282, 283,
884.
Beauchamp/Pohlman/Chapman, at University
of Illinois: 89, 90, 355.
Behrman: 95, 936.
Conley/Radzow: 195.
Cooper: 197.
CSX-1 Music Machine, at University of
Illinois: 229, 383, 515.
Electric Music Box, Buchla/Friedman: 130,

150, 178.
Electronic Music Studio, London: 309,
1013, 1014, 1015.
Electronic Music Studio, Stockholm: 146,
519, 965, 966.
Franco, at Oberlin Conservatory: 620.
Gabura/Ciamaga: 284, 285.
Gonsalves: 210.
GROOVE, Mathews/Moore, at Bell Laboratories:
289, 550, 555, 566, 567, 568, 569, 612.
Hampshire College, Mass: 323.
HYBRID systems I-IV, Kobrin: 89, 90, 355,
425, 426, 453, 455, 456, 459, 817.
Institute of Sonology, Utrecht: 903.
ISMUS, Christiansen/White, at Iowa State
University: 819, 962, 963.
Kupper: 481.
LOGO, Truax, at York University: 91, 92,
93.
Michigan State University: 504.
Mintner: 594.
Moog/Chadabe, at Albany, N.Y.: 149, 150,
152.
Moore: 611.
Moore School, University of Penn.: 967.
PLAY, Chadabe/Meyers, at Albany, N.Y.: 152.
Powell: 710.
Rosenboom, at ARC, Vancouver: 209.
Rossum/Wedge: 778.
Rothenberg: 780.
Sal-Mar Construction, Franco/Martirano,
at University of Illinois: 150, 274.
SYCOM, at University of South Florida:
43, 45, 46.

programs. See composition programs; programmed control,
etc.; synthesis programs; and synthesizers,
digital.

psychoacoustics. See perception, studies of.

quantizing error.
562, 563.

random probability processes, simulation of; random
elements in sound synthesis, composition;
stochastic composition.
40, 118, 132, 189, 195, 256, 257, 266, 268,
289, 291, 416, 448, 650, 653, 682, 686, 708,
709, 745, 765, 843, 846, 859, 873, 875, 900,
911, 913, 918, 920, 970, 981, 982, 983, 984,
985, 986, 987, 988, 989, 990, 991, 992, 993,
994, 995, 996, 1000, 1001, 1006, 1008.

recordings, enclosed with articles and books.
42, 62, 125, 128, 268, 572, 739, 743, 762,
875, 977, 915, 955, 978, 983, 994.

recordings, reviews of.
217, 232, 522, 523, 525, 878.

reverberation, digital simulation of.
8, 174, 198, 509, 627, 660,

rhythmic operations.
46, 152, 290, 298, 550, 719, 728, 840.

sample rate, sampling theorem.
104, 154, 563, 570, 614, 662, 856, 873.

serial operations, computations of.
58, 60, 61, 62, 68, 144, 163, 396, 398, 404,
412, 449, 458, 511, 583, 719, 766, 767, 810.

signal processing, digital.
6, 322, 432, 613, 614, 627, 783, 784, 799,
860.

sine summation synthesis. See Fourier synthesis.

speech synthesis programs, used in music.
145, 197, 214, 230, 231, 232, 308, 432ff.,

437, 438, 488, 505, 553, 558, 579, 600, 605,
625, 628, 629, 630, 651, 676, 677, 678, 679,
830, 831, 904, 905, 906, 908, 946, 974, 979.

stochastic composition. See random, etc.

synthesis programs for direct sound generation.
general discussion: 56, 88, 96, 146, 150,
150, 165, 172, 174, 238, 247, 249, 268, 272,
278, 285, 314, 315, 319, 365, 366, 370, 371,
374, 377, 378, 379, 419, 483, 542, 544, 546,
549, 554, 584, 646, 647, 651, 768, 791, 844,
845, 847, 928.
MUSIC IV: 233, 337, 402, 451, 546, 551, 552,
559, 560, 561, 571, 572, 620, 725, 761, 762,
763, 766, 873, 875, 909, 910, 911, 912, 913.
MUSIC V: 41, 110, 111, 144, 145, 239, 251,
337, 420, 421, 528, 533, 563, 569, 620, 719,
731, 739, 740, 742, 748, 756, 951.
Adaptations of MUSIC IV and MUSIC V: 187, 188,
402, 405, 406, 533-535, 537, 839, 840, 841,
842, 947, 972, 973.
MUSIC 360: 201, 937, 939, 942, 943.
MUSIC7: 401, 404, 407, 408, 581.
other programs: 180, 182, 183, 184, 185, 186,
190, 191, 229, 287, 312, 313, 314, 532, 586,
828, 829, 830, 925, 926, 930, 931, 932.
see also: analysis/synthesis; speech synthesis
programs and music.

synthesizers, digital.
general discussion: 134, 769.
specific systems:
Alles/DiGiugno synthesizer: 8, 9, 10, 11,
70, 94, 96, 218, 219, 503, 528, 770, 822,
823, 856, 955, 956.
CME synthesizer: 310.
Dartmouth synthesizer: 14, 15, 27, 522.
Dworak/Parker system: 237.
Easton synthesizer: 238.
EGG synthesizer: 17, 18, 114, 115, 116,

265

326ff., 329, 330, 501, 539, 540.
Mitsubishi Corp. synthesizer: 345.
MITSYN, at M.I.T.: 148, 343, 344, 860, 939.
Moore synthesizer: 627.
Samson synthesizer: 627, 790.
Smoliar, at University of Penn.: 855.
SSSP synthesizer, at University of Toronto: 140, 142, 255.
Tempelaars/Kaegi system, at University of Utrecht: 904, 905, 906, 908.
Twang, at Xerox Corp. Palo Alto Research Center: 443, 796.
University of Mass. system: 782.
see also: waveform generators, digital.

technology, arts and.
26, 53, 54, 106, 126, 127, 128, 151, 166, 176, 212, 262, 396, 399, 410, 439, 448, 514, 578, 599, 603, 606, 686, 718, 732, 733, 736, 772, 808, 813, 824, 825, 826, 889, 891, 893, 922, 934, 980, 1003, 1006, 1007.

temperaments.
computations of frequencies for various equal-tempered scales: 730, 766, 767, 871.
synthesis of various equal-tempered scales through hybrid or digital systems: 2, 199, 331, 362, 373, 647, 648, 685, 691, 930.
see also: tunings.

textbooks.
28, 241, 401, 441, 563, 806, 996.

touch-sensitive keyboards.
9, 10, 11, 18, 237, 261, 655.

tunings.
just intonation, calculations of: 425, 426, 930.

    synthesis by hybrid or digital means of
    various tunings: 2, 331, 647, 665.
    see also: temperaments.

waveform generators, digital.
    8, 9, 101, 133, 153, 175, 218, 616, 711,
    856, 928.

Names.

Entries listed below are only those names which
appear in locations other than the numbered,
alphabetical listing of authors.

Adorno, Theodore. 339, 889.
Aharonian, Coriun. 639, 825.
Alles, H. G. 70, 94, 503, 528, 756, 770, 822.
Appleton, Jon. 522, 639, 825, 936.
Babbitt, Milton. 798, 867.
Baker, R. A. 448, 650.
Barbaud, Pierre. 58, 482, 529, 530, 607, 650, 896, 923.
Bauer-Mengelberg, Stefan. 246.
Barbut, M. 242.
Beauchamp, James W. 268, 394, 395.
Behrman, David. 936.
Belar, Herbert. 63.
Birtwhistle, Harrison. 309.
Bodin, Lars-Gunnar. 522.
Boeswillwald, Pierre. 639, 825.
Brook, Barry S. 192.
Brün, Herbert. 212, 268, 446, 448, 512, 809, 936.
Brunson, William. 522.
Buchla, Don. 42, 45, 150, 819, 963.
Buxton, William. 639, 825.
Byrd, Donald. 144, 221-228.

Hiller, Lejaren. 44, 150, 268, 448, 481, 512, 607, 622, 650, 688, 700, 732, 806, 808, 961.
Howe, Hubert S. 296, 581, 806.
Isaacson, L. M. 448, 622, 650, 688, 806, 961.
Ives, Charles. 46.
Kaegi, Werner. 175, 905ff.
Kassler, Michael. 999.
Kobrin, Ed. 221-228, 425, 426, 817, 879.
Koenig, G. M. 212, 339, 482, 650, 949.
Kotonski, W. 639, 825.
Krellman, Hanspeter. 992.
Kupper, Leo. 639.
Lachartre, N. 482.
Laske, O. 221-228.
Lauckner, Kurt. 193.
Layzer, A. 409.
Lefkoff, Gerald. 827.
Leibig, Bruce. 310.
Lewin, David. 448, 547.
Ligeti, G. 339.
Mâche, François Bernard. 992.
MacInnis, Donald. 221-228, 581.
Martirano, Salvatore. 150, 274.
Mathews, Max V. 150, 221-228, 233, 239, 268, 288, 289, 319, 402, 420, 421, 448, 451, 482, 599, 607, 620, 688, 719, 727, 739, 761, 762, 768, 806, 873, 877, 1010.
McKee, William. 525.
Ménard, Phillippe. 639, 825.
Meyer-Eppler, Werner. 339.
Moles, A. A. 482, 733, 756, 889.
Moog, Robert. 45, 149, 902.
Moore, F. R. 627.
Moorer, James. 509, 846.
Morrill, Dexter. 523.
Nelson, Gary. 221-228.
O'Beirne, T. H. 448, 732.
Olive, Joseph P. 525.
Olson, Harry F. 63.
Packer, Leo S. 192.

270

Studios, centers of activity

904, 905, 906, 907, 908, 925, 926, 928, 932, 949, 950, 951, 952.

Norway. Oslo. University of Norway. 178, 251.

Poland. Warsaw. 131, 256, 257, 472, 717, 826, 893, 1005, 1006.

Sweden. Stockholm. Elektronmusikstudion (EMS), Sveriges Radio. 105, 146, 417, 446, 519, 935, 951, 965, 966.

Switzerland. Gravesano. Elektroakustisches Experimental-studio Hermann Scherchen. 598, 985.

United Kingdom. Cambridge. 155, 243, 859.
U.K. Fairseat/Wrothram. Oramics Studio. 658.
U.K. London. Electronic Music Studio (EMS), Inc. (Zinovieff). 106, 167, 168, 243, 309, 789, 951, 1013, 1014, 1015.
U.K. Southampton. Southampton University. 337.
U.K. Other locations, not identified. 647, 648, 649, 668, 669, 924, 979.

U.S.A. California. Berkeley. 103.
U.S.A. California. Los Angeles. University of California (UCLA). 268, 873, 874, 875.
U.S.A. California. Oakland. Mills College. 210.
U.S.A. California. Palo Alto. Xerox Corporation Palo Alto Research Center. 443, 795, 796.
U.S.A. California. San Diego. Center for Music Experiment, University of California at La Jolla. 310, 453, 459, 755, 817.
U.S.A. California. San Francisco. (Samson). 790.
U.S.A. California. Stanford. Stanford University. 42, 169, 170, 171, 172, 174, 221ff., 300, 301, 302, 303, 621, 623, 624, 625, 627, 628, 630, 635-637, 783, 784, 839, 840, 841, 842, 951, 976, 978.
U.S.A. Connecticut. New Haven. Yale University. 282, 830.

U.S.A. Florida. Tampa. University of South Florida.
43, 45, 46.
U.S.A. Illinois. Argonne. Argonne National Laboratories.
180, 268, 405, 761, 762, 763.
U.S.A. Illinois. Chicago. Art Institute of Chicago.
236.
U.S.A. Illinois. Chicago. (Kobrin).
221ff., 425, 426, 454, 455, 456, 457, 879.
U.S.A. Illinois. Chicago. Northwestern University.
458.
U.S.A. Illinois. Urbana. University of Illinois,
Experimental Music Studio.   50, 51, 72-76,
79, 82-84, 89, 90, 108, 113, 123, 125, 128,
221ff., 229, 268, 274, 277, 280, 314, 315,
356-359, 361, 362, 363-370, 372, 373, 374,
375, 376, 377, 378-389, 446, 482, 512, 515,
516, 518, 582, 588, 622, 650, 659-662, 688,
700, 728, 786, 808, 951, 961, 995, 996.
U.S.A. Indiana. Bloomington. Indiana University.   143,
144, 190, 191, 221ff., 708, 765, 977, 986.
U.S.A. Indiana. South Bend. Indiana University.   342.
U.S.A. Iowa. Ames. Iowa State University.   175, 819,
962, 963.
U.S.A. Iowa. Iowa City. University of Iowa.   594.
U.S.A. Maine. Brunswick. Bowdoin College.   766, 767,
768.
U.S.A. Massachussetts. Amherst. University of Massa-
chussetts.   782.
U.S.A. Massachussetts. Cambridge. Harvard University.
831.
U.S.A. Massachussetts. Cambridge. Massachussetts
Institute of Technology.   93, 148, 201, 299,
322, 343, 344, 422, 525, 526, 527, 542, 543,
806, 831, 848, 849, 851, 854, 860, '861, 939,
940, 941, 942, 943.
U.S.A. Massachussetts. Hadley. Hampshire College. 323.
U.S.A. Michigan. Ann Arbor. University of Michigan.
937, 938.
U.S.A. Michigan. Lansing. Michigan State University.
504, 505, 957.
U.S.A. New Hampshire. Durham. University of New Hampshire.